Vocabulary

The
**READING
PUZZLE**

Elaine K. McEwan
Val Bresnahan

CORWIN PRESS
Classroom

For information:

Corwin Press
A SAGE Company
2455 Teller Road
Thousand Oaks, California 91320
CorwinPress.com

SAGE, Ltd.
1 Oliver's Yard
55 City Road
London EC1Y 1SP
United Kingdom

SAGE India Pvt. Ltd.
B 1/I 1 Mohan Cooperative
Industrial Area
Mathura Road, New Delhi
India 110 044

SAGE Asia-Pacific Pvt. Ltd.
33 Pekin Street #02-01
Far East Square
Singapore 048763

Printed in the United States of America.

ISBN: 978-1-4129-5822-6

This book is printed on acid-free paper.

08 09 10 11 12 10 9 8 7 6 5 4 3 2 1

Executive Editor: Kathleen Hex
Managing Developmental Editor: Christine Hood
Editorial Assistant: Anne O'Dell
Developmental Writer: Val Bresnahan
Developmental Editor: Joellyn Cicciarelli
Art Director: Anthony D. Paular
Design Project Manager: Jeffrey Stith
Cover Designers: Michael Dubowe and Jeffrey Stith
Illustrator: Mary Rojas
Design Consultant: The Development Source

GRADES **K-3**

The **READING PUZZLE**

TABLE OF CONTENTS

Introduction 4

Put It Into Practice 5

Choosing Appropriate Read-Alouds 8

Word Selection and Definition 11

Take Five 19

CHAPTER 1
Extensive Reading Lessons
Activities and reproducibles

Extensive Reading Lessons 24

CHAPTER 2
Vocabulary Instruction Lessons
Activities

Vocabulary Instruction Lessons 39

CHAPTER 3
Strategy Lessons
Activities and reproducibles

Strategy Lessons 61

CHAPTER 4
Word Awareness Lessons
Activities and reproducibles

Word Awareness Lessons 84

References 96

Introduction

Are you ready to catch students who are "falling through the cracks"? Are you ready to teach them all to read? While it is often easy to identify at-risk students, teaching them can be a challenge. The challenge is often due to critical variables over which teachers have no control, including IQ level, early literacy experiences, socioeconomic status, or the educational level of parents or guardians. The good news is that while you cannot change many things, you can change how you teach. You can instruct in a manner that will enable *all* students to learn.

Because vocabulary has been identified by the National Reading Panel (2000) as one of the critical areas of reading instruction, this book focuses on vocabulary instruction for all students, especially those whose underdeveloped word knowledge negatively impacts their academic performance. This underperformance is characterized by a partial knowledge of word meanings, confusion of words with similar sounds, and limited knowledge of how and when words are typically used. To help at-risk students, several essential instructional factors must be consciously addressed.

The first essential factor for teaching at-risk students is instructional planning and behavior. "Choosing Appropriate Read-Alouds" (pages 8–10) assists you in choosing books at the appropriate listening comprehension level so children's vocabulary development is maximized. "Word Selection and Definition" (pages 11–18) helps you choose words and plan for vocabulary instruction. Teaching behaviors are explained in "Take Five" (pages 19–23) and are woven into the remaining sections of this book.

Four additional factors for comprehensive vocabulary teaching are the following: extensive reading, direct instruction of important individual words, teaching word-learning strategies, and fostering word consciousness (Feldman & Kinsella, 2002). The remainder of this book addresses each essential factor.

With the help of this resource, you can provide a thorough, well-balanced vocabulary program so that all students are reading and none are left behind.

978-1-4129-5822-6

Put It Into Practice

With the mandate to leave no child behind (No Child Left Behind, NCLB) and the approaching deadline of 2014 for all students to be proficient in reading, school districts and teachers at every grade level are working diligently to improve the reading skills of all their students.

The National Reading Panel (2000) identified five areas that increase students' reading ability: phonemic awareness, the alphabetic principle, fluency, vocabulary, and reading comprehension. After third grade, the reading gap is thought to be primarily a vocabulary gap. If students can decode words but still have comprehension difficulties, the culprit is often the inability to understand word meaning—a vocabulary deficit. If students do not know the meaning of the majority (95%) of the words in a paragraph, passage, or story, they will have great difficulty understanding what they are reading.

Strategies used to increase vocabulary skills are an important piece of The Reading Puzzle. The Reading Puzzle is a way of organizing and understanding reading instruction, as introduced in my book, *Teach Them All to Read: Catching the Kids Who Fall Through the Cracks* (2002). The puzzle contains the essential reading skills that students need to master in order to become literate at every grade level. *The Reading Puzzle, Grades K–3* series focuses on five of these skills: Phonics, Phonemic Awareness, Fluency, Comprehension, and Vocabulary.

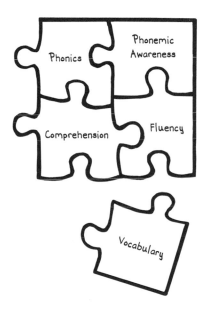

In the earlier grades, vocabulary knowledge refers to the number of words in the student's lexicon, or oral vocabulary, rather than the number of words recognized in print. Reading, or recognizing words in print, is built upon a strong oral language base. However, not all children arrive at school prepared with an adequate oral vocabulary.

While the average child enters kindergarten with a vocabulary of approximately 5,000 words, children from economically disadvantaged homes or from homes in which little or no English is spoken, enter school knowing far fewer words (Blachowitcz, Fisher, & Watts-Taffe, 2005). These linguistically disadvantaged students suffer from partial knowledge of word meanings, confusion over similar sounding words, and limited knowledge of how and when to use words (Moats, 2001). An initial vocabulary deficit puts at-risk students at a tremendous academic and social disadvantage. One of the largest factors negatively influencing reading performance is lack of vocabulary knowledge (Chall, Jacobs, & Baldwin, 1990). In addition, lack of adequate vocabulary knowledge affects a student's ability to function in social as well as academic classroom routines.

Fortunately, classrooms are highly verbal environments. With targeted and direct vocabulary instruction, students with language difficulties, English language learners, economically disadvantaged students, and students with learning disabilities can all become better readers and better all-around students.

This book has been designed to put theory and research into practice and provide students with the targeted and direct vocabulary instruction they need.

Choosing Appropriate Read-Alouds

This section helps you choose vocabulary-building books that students can learn from as well as enjoy.

Word Selection and Definition

This section provides you with concrete ways to select vocabulary words and plan lessons.

Take Five

This section includes presentation techniques so you can make the most of each lesson and provide an atmosphere in which all students can learn.

Chapter 1: Extensive Reading Lessons

This chapter focuses on ways for students to improve their vocabulary in a natural way through reading and listening to stories. Extensive reading has long been thought to improve students' vocabulary. Listening to vocabulary is important because research has shown students are unlikely to substantially increase their vocabularies through independent reading before third grade.

Chapter 2: Vocabulary Instruction Lessons

This chapter is dedicated to direct instruction of vocabulary words and contains a multitude of activities. These activities should be presented in sequence, as one activity builds upon the next. Through this approach, young and at-risk learners are given repeated practice in a variety of contexts, a required strategy for effective vocabulary acquisition.

I wonder what the word "rehearsed" means?

978-1-4129-5822-6

Chapter 3: Strategy Lessons

This chapter provides the best practices of good readers. Young learners, at-risk learners, and struggling readers should be taught these strategies explicitly and in order with repeated practice. Some of these strategies include using picture clues, context clues, prefixes, suffixes, and multiple-meaning words to determine meaning.

Chapter 4: Word Awareness Lessons

This chapter focuses on increasing word consciousness. Typically, at-risk learners are not aware of the words around them. They do not pay attention to unfamiliar words while they read or listen to others speak. This final chapter provides activities to increase word awareness in all language tasks: listening, speaking, reading, and writing. Studies have shown that children's vocabularies increase at a rate of 3,000 words/year or about six to eight words/day (Nagy & Anderson, 1984). Students need direct experience with oral and written language to achieve this type of growth. They must become enthralled with the words around them. Students learn new words by engaging in conversations with adults, listening to adults read to them, and by reading on their own. Even television can be the source of new vocabulary. Students learn new words on their own when they become fascinated by words.

978-1-4129-5822-6

Choosing Appropriate Read-Alouds

Some students enter kindergarten with less listening comprehension and a more limited reading vocabulary than other students. Unless listening comprehension and vocabulary levels are significantly augmented, these students will lag behind in reading, writing, listening, speaking, and content-area learning. The good news is that chances for successfully addressing listening comprehension and vocabulary differences are greatest in the prekindergarten through early primary years.

Preschool to third-grade students often do not learn new vocabulary from independent reading. Research has shown, however, that they can learn new vocabulary while listening to stories. When considered as part of vocabulary instruction, reading aloud to students can increase vocabulary rather than simply entertain. To do this, you must structure read-aloud sessions that focus specifically on vocabulary. The effectiveness of read-aloud stories depends upon the books chosen, the words selected for explicit instruction, and the language of discussion.

Book Selection

Teachers often have a plethora of favorite books that they read countless times to students. However, many children's picture books contain sentence structure and vocabulary that are well beyond the listening level of struggling students, students with impoverished vocabulary and language levels, and English language learners. In order for these students to expand their skills in listening comprehension as well as vocabulary, attention must be given to story level. Reading experts (Hickman, Pollard-Durodol, & Vaughn, 2004) recommend the following when selecting books for reading aloud:

- Select books that are only one to two levels above students' grade placement level.

- Group three to four books together by theme.

- Break longer stories into smaller units, such as passages of 200–250 words to be read at one sitting.

- Select only two or three words per every 250 words for vocabulary development.

Readability

Children's picture books are often assumed to be at an appropriate level for prekindergarten through the early primary grades. However, many stories contain unfamiliar words and complex sentence structures that make listening comprehension and vocabulary development difficult. One way to determine a book's level is to complete a readability analysis. Two readability formulas, Spache and Dale-Chall, use sentence length and specific words in determining the level of a passage. These formulas are currently available free of charge at the Intervention Central Web site: *http://www.interventioncentral.org/htmdocs/tools/okapi/okapi.php.* The basic steps are as follows:

1. Type a 200- to 250-word selection from a picture book's text.

2. Highlight and copy the section.

3. Go to the aforementioned Web site.

4. Put the cursor on the *Text to Be Analyzed* section and paste the text in place.

5. Type the title and author in the sections indicated.

6. Choose a serif font and small font size so all text will be analyzed.

7. Select a formula from the drop-down menu. Spache is intended for primary grades. Dale-Chall formula is used for texts above fourth grade. Texts are often written substantially above the third-grade level, so you may want to run a readability analysis using both formulas.

8. Select additional options. Be sure to choose *Highlight Difficult Words* and *Show Readability Formula*.

9. Choose *Run Readability Formula.* The formula, highlighted difficult words, and average sentence length will appear.

10. Print and save the results.

11. If the text is no more than two years above the current grade placement, it is appropriate to use. If not, do not use this text for vocabulary development at this grade level.

978-1-4129-5822-6

Themes

Reading experts advise selecting several books according to students' interests and based on theme. By grouping together three or four books according to a specific theme, students have many opportunities to encounter and generalize vocabulary across texts, thus providing them with multiple exposures in a variety of contexts.

A thematic text selection provides students with many opportunities to use and extend vocabulary. Specific words from each story can be used. In addition, related words that do not appear in the stories can be introduced and learned. For example, the words *overcome, imagine,* and *terrified* may not appear in picture books chosen for a theme about overcoming fear. Yet, these concepts might be evident across the texts, so the words could be used repeatedly as each book is read, discussed, and compared. Talk to your local librarian to find reference books that organize children's book titles by subject matter. One such reference book is *A to Zoo: Subject Access to Children's Picture Books* by Carolyn Lima (2006).

Small Text Sections

Chances are that you often choose to read an entire story during one lesson. However, dividing a book into smaller sections and reading only parts of a story is often a good idea. Reading smaller sections of 200 to 250 words has a number of advantages for students with limited listening and language skills. By dividing text into smaller units, you can focus on a fewer number of vocabulary words and adequately discuss meaning. Also, by reading shorter, consecutive passages over time, long-term memory is engaged as students maintain story and content comprehension over time. Prolonged reading also provides an opportunity to use vocabulary words during story discussion.

Theme: Friendship

Word Selection and Definition

Intensive, direct vocabulary instruction is critical to produce in-depth vocabulary knowledge. Once you have chosen appropriate books to read aloud and have been provided with students' textbooks and nonfiction reading materials, you must decide which words to teach. If you carefully analyze text and provide a rationale for words to be taught, instructional time will be maximized. Well-planned, explicit vocabulary instruction involves conscientious vocabulary preparation.

Utility Check

One proven method to help you determine which words to target for explicit vocabulary instruction is the utility check. As you consider words, analyze them according to their levels of utility and teach them as suggested below.

Tier I Words

Tier I words are basic words that commonly appear in spoken language and in numerous contexts. Do not spend much time on Tier I words, as most students will likely know them. To assist at-risk learners, provide a common synonym for an unfamiliar Tier I word.

Tier II Words

Tier II words are the words of academic and literary language. Tier II words are found in nonfiction texts across subject areas. They have been referred to as "mortar" words, as they connect different contexts. Students probably will not hear these words used repeatedly in context, and therefore, will not be familiar with them. These words will appear increasingly in academic texts as students move through the grades and should be explicitly taught.

Tier III Words

Tier III words are domain-specific words. They are low-frequency words that do not generalize well. Historical and mathematics terms are examples of Tier III words. While Tier III words are important to building knowledge and conceptual understanding within a specific content area, they rarely appear in general usage. Unfortunately, most teacher guides and textbooks focus solely on Tier III words. To build vocabulary, you must decide which words are Tier III words and briefly explain them, but elaborate only when necessary. Excessive exercises or memorization are not often worthwhile for words with a limited range of use.

Context Check

Experts advise that only two or three words per day can be learned deeply and internalized. However, there can be many other words within a picture book, chapter book, or nonfiction unit that require clarification for understanding the material. Fortunately, there are some guidelines in determining which words should be targeted for direct vocabulary study. Many vocabulary experts suggest the following guidelines:

Important Words

Select words that are important to understanding the text. These words may be found directly in the text, or they may not be in the text but are important to understanding the theme.

Useful Words

Choose words with general utility that are likely to be encountered in the future, such as Tier II words.

Unfamiliar or Confusing Words

Consider teaching words or expressions that may need interpretation, such as multiple-meaning words, abstract nuances, idioms, and metaphoric expressions.

Getting Ready

Follow these steps to determine which vocabulary words you will teach during a specific lesson or unit:

Word Selection and Analysis Chart

BOOK OR UNIT TITLE: _____

CHAPTER/PAGE NUMBERS: _____

Word	Page Number(s)	Tier I	Tier II	Tier III	Multiple-Meaning or Figurative	Critical to Understanding the Text

978-1-4129-5822-6 • © Corwin Press   Reproducible   The Reading Puzzle: Vocabulary • Grades K–3 **17**

1. Select a 200- to 250-word passage from a picture book, chapter book, novel, or nonfiction text.

2. Run a readability formula as described on page 9. Or, if you do not have computer access, read through the selection and look for difficult words. Look for words with which students have had difficulty, such as multisyllabic words.

3. Read the text again. This time, look for figurative language and multiple-meaning words.

4. Use the **Word Selection and Analysis Chart reproducible (page 17)** to list difficult words, multiple-meaning words, and figurative language. Also include the page number of the word or phrase so you can determine how often the word is used and where it is used.

5. Analyze the words you listed. Determine which words are very basic common words (Tier I), high-frequency "mortar" words (Tier II), and domain-specific words (Tier III). Also decide if the word is critical to understanding the text. Put a checkmark in the appropriate column. Some words may have checkmarks in more than one column.

6. Choose two or three words to teach. When selecting Tier II words, focus on vocabulary that can be connected to key themes or ideas in the text and that naturally coincide with discussions and other activities.

Kid-Friendly Definitions, Examples, and Questions

Teachers, not dictionaries, must define new vocabulary for students. A dictionary is often an inappropriate source for young students to learn new, unfamiliar vocabulary. Consider the following:

- Young children often do not have the reading ability needed to understand dictionary entries.

- There are many definitions from which to choose. One has to have a sense of the word to choose the correct definition.

- Reading a definition does not tell how the word is used. Connotation is extremely important.

- Students need numerous examples in context to glean the meaning of a word.

- Dictionary definitions are truncated.

Once you have selected two or three words for explicit vocabulary instruction using the Word Selection and Analysis Chart, go through these planning steps before introducing the words:

Step 1: Write a Kid-Friendly Definition (KFD)

First, locate the most common definition from the dictionary. Note difficult, multisyllabic, multiple-meaning, or repetitive words in the dictionary definition. Replace those difficult words with words students already know. Rewrite the definition using words and sentence structure that are easy to understand. Double-check your KFD. Would a very young student understand this definition? If so, then you've probably created a definition that a diverse student body will readily grasp.

Word	Dictionary Definition	KFD
overcome	To **struggle successfully** against a difficulty or disadvantage	To win after a hard fight
terrified	To be **filled** with **terror**	Very afraid
imagine	To form a **mental picture** of something **not present**	To think of something that isn't real

Step 2: Write Examples

After you have created a KFD, the next step is to write affirmative and negative examples to extend and refine the meaning of the word. The examples you select should be relevant to students' lives. The more familiar the example, the more effective the word learning will be. Use of examples activates background knowledge, which is a critical component of effective learning. Negative examples are effective in narrowing meaning and providing word boundaries.

Word	Affirmative Examples	Negative Examples
terrified	I am terrified of snakes. I'm afraid they will hurt me.	I am not terrified of my sister's pet hamster. I let him crawl on me.
	Some people are terrified of flying in an airplane. They do not want to get on.	Blake loves the dark. He is not terrified to have the lights out.
	The baby rabbit was terrified when it saw a shadow, so it ran away.	Cara is not terrified when the doorbell rings. She knows that the door is locked.

terrified

978-1-4129-5822-6

Step 3: Write Yes/No Questions

After you think of examples to present, craft yes/no questions that will get students' brains thinking. Construct questions that reflect real life and to which students can relate. Begin with obvious sentences that incorporate word definitions.

When presenting yes/no questions, invite young students to give you a thumbs-up for *yes* and a thumbs-down for *no*.

Question Examples

- *If you were hiking and saw bear tracks and heard a growl behind you, would you be terrified?*

- *If you saw a bear in the zoo, would you feel terrified?*

- *Would a terrified person easily fall asleep?*

Word Introduction Plan

To help you create KFDs, examples, and questions that will guide your instruction and help students, use the **Word Introduction Plan reproducible (page 18)**.

Word Introduction Plan

Book or Unit Title	Chapter/Page Numbers
Central Lesson Theme	

Word	Pages

Kid-Friendly Definition (KFD)

KFD Checklist
- ❑ Words are ones students already know
- ❑ Words are easy to understand
- ❑ Succinct definition
- ❑ Demonstrates typical use of word

Relationship to Central Lesson Theme

Affirmative Examples	Negative Examples
1.	1.
2.	2.
3.	3.

Yes/No Questions
1.
2.
3.
4.
5.

Teaching Time

After using the Word Introduction Plan, you are ready to present the new words to students. Follow these steps to present a word:

Step 1

Pronounce the word and have students repeat it after you. Call attention to the number of syllables as well as the spelling. Also point out any unique orthographic features in the word. Use your Word Introduction Plan for Steps 2 through 5.

Step 2

Provide your Kid-Friendly Definition (KFD).

Step 3

Give the three affirmative examples.

Step 4

Give the three negative examples.

Step 5

Ask the yes/no questions that you wrote.

Step 6

Invite students to give their own examples of yes/no questions.

Step 7

Have students in grades two or three record the vocabulary in a Vocabulary Log such as the one found on page 38.

After you introduce a word for the first time, consider using it for the lessons that follow in Chapters 1–4.

Would you be *terrified* during a thunder and lightning storm?

978-1-4129-5822-6

Word Selection and Analysis Chart

BOOK OR UNIT TITLE: _____

CHAPTER/PAGE NUMBERS: _____

Word	Page Number(s)	Tier I	Tier II	Tier III	Multiple-Meaning or Figurative	Critical to Understanding the Text

Word Introduction Plan

Book or Unit Title	Chapter/Page Numbers

Central Lesson Theme	

Word	Pages

Kid-Friendly Definition (KFD)

KFD Checklist

❑ Words are ones students already know

❑ Words are easy to understand

❑ Succinct definition

❑ Demonstrates typical use of word

Relationship to Central Lesson Theme

Affirmative Examples	Negative Examples
1.	1.
2.	2.
3.	3.

Yes/No Questions
1.
2.
3.
4.
5.

Take Five

Preparing for and Presenting Effective Lessons

When teaching, *how* you teach is just as important as *what* you teach. Research has demonstrated again and again that what the teacher does in the classroom directly affects student learning. Your teaching behaviors and presentation techniques are the catalysts for learning.

The five effective presentation techniques included in this resource are advance organizer, active engagement, scaffolded instruction, ongoing practice, and big ideas.

Advance Organizer

An advance organizer is a verbal "road map" for students, so they know where they are going and why they are going there. While higher achievers can often ferret out a lesson's direction and make connections to previously learned material, at-risk learners must be explicitly told. Disorganized students do not automatically make connections from one segment of a lesson to another.

To help students cognitively organize before a lesson, start each class with a predictable routine. Tell students:

- to get ready for some important information
- what they are going to learn
- why they are going to learn it
- how it is connected to what they've learned before
- what behavior is expected of them
- how you are going to assess their learning

Active Engagement

To retain information, students must be active during all phases of learning. Too often at-risk students lose focus and interest, leaving all the work (and the learning) to the high achievers. Teachers unintentionally feed into this by using the typical "raise your hand before speaking" routine. Fortunately, there are several ways to ensure that *all* students are engaged. Some of these strategies include:

Role Play and Physical Response

Students in the primary grades often benefit from using their bodies to pantomime answers or from working in groups to act out answers in small role plays or skits.

Unison/Choral Response

All students respond together on your signal. A signal can be visual, such as a hand drop, or auditory, such as a clap. Unison responses are effective for single-word answers. Be sure to allow a few seconds of think time between asking the question and requiring a response.

Partner Response

Students work in pairs to formulate and share answers. Critical for vocabulary activities, this technique lowers the risk for students who are less sure of themselves. It is often beneficial to partner a high achiever with a middle achiever and a middle achiever with a low achiever. During the lesson, regularly stop, present a question, and ask partners to share answers before you randomly call on them, giving students an opportunity to think about and rehearse their answers.

Dry-Erase Board Response

At the start of class, provide each student with a small dry-erase board, a dry-erase marker, and a cloth. If dry-erase boards are not available at your school, cut large plastic sheets obtained from home improvement stores or use recycled lids from large plastic food storage tubs.

At frequent intervals throughout a lesson, ask students to "board" their responses in drawings, in words, or in word approximations with invented spelling. This action makes students individually accountable for each response yet is less threatening than using paper or giving a verbal response. Tour the room to check answers and gauge how much more practice is needed before moving on. You can also provide individual corrective feedback. For example: *You are almost there!* or *The first part of your answer is correct.*

Note: Because each lesson in this book includes active engagement at several points of instruction, an icon is not included for this presentation technique.

Scaffolded Instruction

Scaffolded instruction refers to providing support at each phase of a lesson so students can learn and become secure in a new skill. With adequate instruction and ongoing feedback from a teacher, new knowledge can be gained and internalized. Following are steps for a scaffolded instruction plan.

Step 1: Teacher Modeling (Watch Me Do It)

At the beginning phase or introduction of the skill, demonstrate how to do the activity while telling students what you're doing. This is the "watch me do it" phase. While performing the activity, talk through each step, showing and explaining. Remember the words *show*, *tell*, and *interact* as a guide to the type of support you should provide at this stage.

Step 2: Teacher and Students Work Together (Do It With Me)

After modeling, work with students while you teach. This is the "do it with me" phase. During this phase, provide support as needed, but gradually withdraw support as students become more proficient. Step in if a student falters and gradually withdraw support.

Step 3: Students Work Independently (On Your Own)

When students are ready to work independently, this is known as the "on your own" phase. During this phase, closely monitor what students are doing. Correct errors immediately to prevent bad habits from forming. Be sure to observe students' level of understanding while providing assistance as needed.

Using scaffolded instruction ("watch me do it," "do it with me," "on your own") enables students to get it right from the start. With clear guidance, they avoid mistakes that interfere with learning and keep their self-esteem intact. Sometimes referred to as "errorless learning," scaffolded instruction is often more effective than reteaching.

Ongoing Practice

How often have you learned something only to forget the concept or process because you were not able to apply the skill repeatedly? Perhaps you were able to successfully complete a task once, but three months later, you forgot some of the steps. For most of us, any skill that we do not routinely apply will most likely be forgotten.

Ongoing Practice for At-Risk Learners

At-risk learners, like all of us, need ongoing practice and review. With repeated practice, students can master and retain concepts, vocabulary, information, and skills. Merely presenting information and moving on to the next skill or vocabulary word is insufficient.

At-risk learners often have difficulty integrating new concepts with previously learned information. You can prevent this by constantly reviewing and integrating. Never leave critical information in the past. If information is important for students to know, be sure it is repeated, revisited, and rehearsed throughout the year.

Remember these words as you plan for repeated practice: *Practice must be **sufficient**, **varied**, **distributed**, and **integrated**.* Following are definitions of these words as they relate to ongoing practice:

- sufficient = good quality and enough to ensure mastery

- varied = uses many learning modalities in a variety of student groupings

- distributed = presented in class and as homework

- integrated = presented within the context of content instruction as well as in isolation

A Word About Assessment Without Sufficient Practice

Avoid presenting concepts followed by immediate assessment because sometimes students appear to have obtained mastery when they have not. In such cases, when the skill is tested again at a later time, students may not have the ability to recall or apply the information or skills. Allow plenty of time for review, practice, and integration before assessing a skill.

978-1-4129-5822-6

Big Idea

As you plan your lessons and get ready to employ advance organizer, active engagement, scaffolded instruction, and ongoing practice, think about the most important ideas and skills you want to instill in your students. Make an effort to streamline what you teach and to focus on critical content.

Critical Streamlining

Critical streamlining is left to you, the teacher, because you know your students best. Do not depend on the curriculum or textbooks, as these might focus on a "succession of forgettable details" (Wallis & Steptoe, 2006) rather than key concepts taught in-depth. Remember that information cannot be retained unless routinely applied. There is simply too much material to be learned at too shallow a depth. At-risk learners cannot begin to master a curriculum that "gallops through a mind-numbing stream of topics and subtopics" (Wallis & Steptoe, 2006).

Lesson Preparation

To effectively teach all students, especially those at risk, trim the content to a manageable amount. Stop galloping and start reflecting. Take stock of the most important big ideas. As you plan lessons, ask yourself these questions:

- If my students only take one idea away from this lesson/unit, what should that be?

- What do I want them to remember ten years from now?

- What am I teaching that has universal application?

- What are the key concepts that I need to cover in-depth?

- How can I relate these key concepts to other lessons I have taught or to other disciplines?

Take Five Summary

By making the Take Five presentation techniques part of your teaching routine, you will have greater impact on your students, especially at-risk learners. Whether you are teaching sixth-grade literature or eighth-grade advanced algebra, world history or plot elements, kindergarten or high school, these instructional behaviors result in more effective teaching and learning.

CHAPTER 1

Extensive Reading Lessons

Let's Listen and Learn

Materials
- butcher-paper banner
- sentence strips
- three 500- to 1,000-word picture books with the same central theme
- book covers

Grade Levels
K–1

Objective
Students will develop new vocabulary as they listen to books that you read aloud.

 **Big Idea**

Background Information
Before reading picture books specifically chosen for building vocabulary, it is important to prepare students. Like you, your students probably have experienced many read-aloud situations in which the story is read to completion. Unless told otherwise, children will be expecting a similar experience. Keep in mind that listening comprehension and vocabulary development are the primary objectives of "Let's Listen and Learn." You may decide to read aloud for enjoyment at other times, but be sure that "Let's Listen and Learn" is a part of your daily instructional routine.

Before you begin, choose three 500- to 1,000-word picture books that revolve around the same central theme. Use the strategies from "Choosing Appropriate Read-Alouds" (pages 8–10) and "Word Selection and Definition" (pages 11–18) to choose appropriate books, to divide the books into instructional sections for reading aloud, and to prepare vocabulary words. Hang a butcher-paper banner on a blank classroom wall. On the banner, write the central theme of the picture books in large letters. Attach the cover of each picture book on the banner with room for sentence strips below. Have ready the three theme-related picture books and blank sentence strips.

Instructional Sequence

 1. Advance Organizer

Tell students:

I am going to start reading to you for a very special reason. The reason is that I want you to listen and learn new words. To be good readers, writers, and speakers someday, you need to know a lot of words and what they mean.

You are going to do this by listening to stories. I am not going to read a whole story at one time. I will read only a short part of the story. Each part will have two or three words that we will study. We will practice these words every day. On the last day, I will read the whole story from start to finish.

Stand up if a grown-up has ever read to you. Now sit down. What stories did you hear? Did you listen carefully? I expect you to listen quietly while I read. Who can show me what good listening behavior looks like? I also will expect you to pay attention to the new words. I will expect you to remember these words and to use them when you talk about the story.

I will put the new words on sentence strips. I do not expect you to be able to read or spell the words, but I do want you to see the letters in the words, especially the beginning letters. I want you to notice the length of the word. I want you to be able to say all the sounds in the word.

We will put the words on a banner under a picture of the book cover. We will only read one or two books a week, but we will learn lots and lots of words. Who can remember something I just said? Tell your partner what you remember.

2. Scaffolded Instruction

Model Understanding Theme

Explain to students the meaning of the word *theme* as it relates to a story. Explain that books have big ideas (themes) and small ideas (main ideas and details). Give examples as students relate to a book they know.

Point to the theme banner and read aloud the words. Point out the covers of the three theme-related picture books you will read for vocabulary development. Relate the books' theme to students' lives.

Modeling Example *Did you know that books can be about big ideas and small ideas? Think about the book* Green Eggs and Ham. *This book has big ideas and small ideas. Some of the small ideas in this book are that there is a man named Sam, and that Sam likes to eat green eggs and ham. But what is the big idea? Some people might say that the big idea in this book is that we shouldn't be afraid to try new things. The big idea in a book is called the theme.*

I have picked three books and they all have the same big idea, the same theme. Look at the banner. It says "Overcoming Fear." That is the theme of the books whose covers you see displayed on the banner. To overcome something means to win after a hard struggle. If you overcome fear, you win over fear. You are not afraid anymore. Have you ever been afraid but got over it? Tell a friend about a time when you were afraid but you overcame it—you did something that made you not afraid anymore.

Model Picture Book Introduction

Display the first picture book. Read aloud the title and author. Summarize the story and tell how it relates to the theme. Explain that you will only read aloud part of the story, and you have chosen two or three new words from that part of the story to study. Each time you read a new section of the book, you will introduce two or three new words.

978-1-4129-5822-6

Do It With Me

Book One, Part One Follow the "Teaching Time" steps (page 16) to introduce the two or three vocabulary words you have chosen from the first part of the first picture book. Write the words on sentence strips and post them on the theme banner under the book's displayed cover.

Read aloud the first section of the first picture book, inviting students to listen carefully for the new words. After reading, ask students to retell, role-play, or perform a skit to share the story's plot to this point.

Review the new words by having students use each word in a sentence related to the story. Kindergarten students might enjoy pantomiming the words' meanings.

Reread the section. Tell students to give a thumbs-up when they hear a vocabulary word. Then remind students that they will hear the next section of the story tomorrow.

Book One, Part Two and Beyond Repeat the vocabulary instruction procedure as you read each section of the book on subsequent days, introducing two or three new vocabulary words for each day/section.

On the day after you finish reading the last part of the book, review all the vocabulary words posted on the banner. Review the theme words and discuss how the book relates to the theme. Reread the entire story from start to finish. Tell students to give a thumbs-up when they hear a vocabulary word.

Review all the vocabulary words posted on the banner, and have students use the words as they retell, role-play, or perform a skit to summarize the story.

Books Two and Three Continue the format from book one with the other books. Resist the temptation to finish a book in one session. When you can, incorporate previous vocabulary words as you read the rest of the books.

 ## 3. Ongoing Practice

As students show the need for more intensive vocabulary instruction with certain words, consider using Chapter 2, "Vocabulary Instruction Lessons" (pages 39–60.)

Once you finish vocabulary instruction using the three picture books of the first theme, choose a new theme and books and repeat the "Let's Listen and Learn" activities throughout the year. If you have room, keep completed banners posted and refer to the words throughout the year as the class listens, speaks, reads, and writes.

Just Right Checklist

Materials

- Just Right Checklist reproducible
- picture books or easy chapter books for modeling book selection
- student fiction and nonfiction picture books or easy chapter books
- scissors
- glue or tape

Grade Levels
2–3

Objective
Students will select books that they can read independently.

 **Big Idea**

Background Information

Estimates indicate that young children can acquire and retain two or three words per day through direct, explicit, contextualized instruction. Given a 180-day school year, that comes to 360–540 words per year, a far cry from the vast number of words necessary for adequate vocabulary growth.

In addition to direct, explicit instruction of word meanings, teachers should encourage students who can read independently to read more. To accomplish this while avoiding boredom and frustration, students must be taught how to select books at their appropriate independent reading level. (If students cannot read independently, use the "Let's Listen and Learn" lesson [pages 24–27] to develop vocabulary through extensive reading.)

Reading a book that is "just right" means that students read well enough independently to understand it. There are three components to reading at the "just right" level:

- accurate decoding of 95% of the words or better
- knowledge of at least 90% of the words
- comprehension of at least 75% of the words

Frequently, student reading selections are written above the "just right" level of at-risk readers. Therefore, students must be explicitly taught how to select appropriate books while enjoying incentives that encourage them to read.

Instructional Sequence

 1. Advance Organizer

Tell students:

Heads up for something important! You are all learning to read, and today you are going to learn how to choose books that you can understand and enjoy. To learn the meanings of new words, you must read a lot, but you must read books that are just right for you.

I am going to teach you a new strategy to help you find books that are at a "just right" level for you. The books will not be too easy, and they will not be too hard. Everyone's "just right" level is different. First, I will show you the steps. Then, you will do the steps with me. Finally, you will try them on your own with your leisure reading books. I will check how you are doing by inviting you to read to me.

 2. Scaffolded Instruction

Model

Before modeling, give students a copy of the **Just Right Checklist reproducible (page 31)**. Go through each step on the checklist thoroughly and explicitly, thinking aloud and describing what you are doing as you go through each step. Model both positive and negative examples so students are aware that even good readers are selective about what they read. Show students how to cut out the bookmark, fold it down the middle, and glue or tape it together.

Modeling Example *The steps for finding "just right" books are on this checklist. Follow along on the checklist as I show you how to do it. First, I have to pick a book that looks interesting to me. It is* Ramona the Pest, *written by Beverly Cleary. She has written many books for children, including* Henry Huggins, *so I know she is a good writer. I am going to look at the front and back of the book. The title and the cover picture look interesting. On the back there is a short summary of the book. I am going to read it to help me decide if it interests me. So far, it looks like I will like this book.*

Date:
March 22, 2008

Name:
Karina Lopez

Book Title:
Ramona the Pest

☑ This is a "just right" book for me.

❑ This is not a "just right" book for me.

Teacher or Parent Signature
Mr. Hogan

1. Pick a book. Read the title and front and back covers.
2. Look at the pages. Are the words too hard? If so, get a new book.
3. Choose three parts to test. Count 20 words in each part.
4. "Whisper-read" the first part.
5. Mark words you don't know. (Do not count people's names.)
6. If you missed more than one word, the part was too hard.
7. Close the book and tell yourself what you just read.
8. If you could not tell what the book was about, the part was too hard.
9. Repeat Steps 4 through 8 for the middle and the ending parts of the book.
10. If you missed one word or less in each part, and you could tell about the story, the book is just right. Enjoy!

Next, I am going to look through the book for the size of the print and the pictures. There aren't too many words, and there are a lot of pictures, so I think I can go on to the next step. I will choose three spots in the book to test—one near the beginning, one near the middle, and one near the end. Now I have to count about 20 words in the first section, or about three lines of text. I will "whisper-read" those words. I have to mark any words I don't understand, but I can skip people's names. Here I go. Now I will look away from the section and tell myself what I just read. I did pretty well! I only missed one word when I was reading, and I understood what I read.

Now I will repeat this with the other two parts of the book. None of the sections were too hard, so this book is just right. I can read it! Now I will record the information on the checklist. If I were a student like you, my teacher or a parent would sign at the bottom.

Do It With Me

Provide a variety of fiction and nonfiction picture books or easy chapter books of different levels and genres for students to examine and use as the subject of their checklist recording. It may be necessary to go through the steps several times until students are comfortable with the sequence.

Teacher Script Example *I am going to give you a book from the library cart. You each will have a different book. We are going to walk through the "just right" steps together. I will read the step, and you will do what the step says to do.*

On Your Own

Provide time for students to choose and survey a variety of fiction and nonfiction picture books or easy chapter books from the library cart. Give them plenty of time to use the Just Right Checklist as a guide. Tour the room to offer guidance in reading and understanding the steps for choosing a book. Once students choose a book that they feel is just right, invite them to read aloud a short excerpt to you. Discuss each student's choice and redirect if necessary.

Teacher Script Example *Now it's your turn. Take some time with the books and follow the "just right" steps. Ask questions if you do not understand one or more of the steps. When you are ready and have chosen a book, bring it to me and read it aloud. We will talk about whether or not the book seems like a good fit.*

Just Right Checklist

Just Right! ✓

Date:

_____

Name:

_____

Book Title:

_____

❏ This is a "just right" book for me.

❏ This is not a "just right" book for me.

Teacher or Parent Signature

_____

1. Pick a book. Read the title and front and back covers.

2. Look at the pages. Are the words too hard? If so, get a new book.

3. Choose three parts to test. Count 20 words in each part.

4. "Whisper-read" the first part.

5. Mark words you don't know. (Do not count people's names.)

6. If you missed more than one word, the part was too hard.

7. Close the book and tell yourself what you just read.

8. If you could not tell what the book was about, the part was too hard.

9. Repeat Steps 4 through 8 for the middle and the ending parts of the book.

10. If you missed one word or less in each part, and you could tell about the story, the book is just right. Enjoy!

Reading Railroad

Materials

- Reading Railroad reproducible
- crayons or markers
- scissors
- tape
- picture books

Grade Levels

K–3

Objective

Students will read or listen to reading for a required number of minutes per week and record progress on an expanding class chart.

Big Idea

Background Information

One proven way to improve word knowledge is through extensive reading. In the "Let's Listen and Learn" lesson, students learned to listen carefully to theme-related books. In the "Just Right Checklist" lesson, students learned to choose books for independent reading. Once one of these routines is established, you can create a reading accountability/ incentive system. One incentive is for the class to add to a growing "train" of book titles as they read or listen to books.

In advance, use crayons or markers to decorate the engine photocopied from the **Reading Railroad reproducible (page 34)**. Post the engine on the classroom wall in a place where other railroad cars can be added behind it. Make several copies of the railroad car on the reproducible so they are ready for students to complete and post behind the engine.

Instructional Sequence

 ## 1. Advance Organizer
Tell students:

For you to learn a lot of new words, you must read books that are just right for you and listen carefully as grown-ups read aloud to you or speak to you. Everyone knows that it takes a lot of practice to learn to ride a bike. The same is true for learning new words. You must practice reading and listening.

Every day we will have "reading railroad" time. This is our time to listen to or read stories with the sole purpose of learning new words. Every time I finish reading you a book, or when one of you finishes reading a book on your own, I will add a car to our train. I'd like to see if we can build a train that goes all the way around the room and out into the hall. Do you think we can reach that far? I can't wait to get started! Once we add 100 cars to the train, the class will receive a reward.

 ## 2. Scaffolded Instruction

Model
Read aloud a brief picture book. Think aloud as you complete the information on a train car cut from the Reading Railroad reproducible.

Do It With Me
Have students work with you to decorate the car and tape it onto the wall behind the engine you have already posted.

3. Ongoing Practice
Read to students, or have students read independently in class. Each time a book is finished, fill in the information on a car cutout, decorate the car, and add it to the wall. When your class reaches 100 books read and posted, provide students with a reward. Add to the train throughout the year, and challenge students to make a train that reaches a great distance.

Reading Railroad

All Aboard the
Reading Railroad

How many books
can we read?

Book Title: _____

Author: _____

Read by: _____

Favorite Word from Book: _____

Reproducible   978-1-4129-5822-6 • © Corwin Press

Vocabulary Log

Grade Levels
2–3

Objective
Student will develop independence in vocabulary acquisition by selecting unfamiliar words from their own independent reading.

 Big Idea

Background Information

Novice readers have a tendency to skip words that are unfamiliar or are familiar but have alternate meanings. Typically, at-risk readers struggle so much with decoding that they have little energy left to locate words such as these in reference sources. Thankfully, when students read books that are at their "just right" levels, they can often read with enough fluency to comprehend as well as to define unfamiliar words or words that are used in a new context.

Before assigning the following activity, be sure you have taught students how to locate unfamiliar words. The **Vocabulary Log reproducible (page 38)** requires students to locate one vocabulary word for each reading session. This activity is intentionally brief to encourage students to read and locate words without becoming overwhelmed.

Materials
- Vocabulary Log reproducible
- transparency of Vocabulary Log reproducible
- transparencies for reading selection exerpts
- overhead projector, marker

Instructional Sequence

1. Advance Organizer
Tell students:

We are going to begin a daily reading activity to help you find words that are new to you in some way. To do this, you will record words on a chart. To learn new words, you must become aware of words that you have never seen before or words that you have seen but have meanings you don't understand. You will be finding words on your own in the "just right" books that you are reading.

As you read to yourself, you should be on the lookout for new words. When you find a new word, you will write the word, the page number on which it appears, the entire sentence in which it appears, and what you think the meaning of the word might be.

Model

Before modeling, give students a copy of the Vocabulary Log reproducible. Review the example on the top half of the reproducible and explain each element.

Then display a transparency showing a section from a reading selection, such as an easy chapter book. Invite students to read aloud the section with you. Use an overhead marker (to simulate a student pencil) to track as you read so students know where to look. When you come to an unusual word, underline it. Be sure to think aloud as you go through the excerpt. Continue to read, underlining unusual words. Call attention to a word that is common but used in a unique way.

When you're done, read all the words that you underlined. Choose one word. Replace the reading selection transparency with a Vocabulary Log transparency. Model how to return to the text, locate the word, touch it, say it, and spell it aloud. Return to the chart and write the word as you say the letters aloud. Go back to double-check the word in the text. Complete the chart while thinking aloud.

Do It With Me

Go through the steps another time with a different excerpt. This time ask students to help you with the steps. Repeat with other excerpts to provide additional scaffolding.

On Your Own

During the same instructional session, have students open a "just right" book. Ask them to work in pairs first. Have them read with a partner and jointly select words. Walk around the room, providing assistance as needed. After students have demonstrated mastery working in pairs, have them work independently.

 ## 3. Ongoing Practice

Assign this activity as homework after students have demonstrated mastery working independently.

Vocabulary Log

Example
Book Title: *A to Z Mysteries: The Unwilling Umpire*

Day/Date	Word	Page Number	Exact Sentence
Monday Jan. 29	display	4	Six of Mr. Pool's baseballs were on display.

Book Title: _____

Day/Date	Word	Page Number	Exact Sentence

CHAPTER 2

Vocabulary Instruction Lessons

Picture/Word Sort

Grade Levels
K–1

Objective
Students will categorize common words into groupings.

 **Big Idea**

Background Information

Materials
- two 3' pieces of yarn
- color and number picture/word vocabulary cards (picture on one side, word on the other)
- variety of additional picture/word vocabulary cards (picture on one side, word on the other)

Leading experts in education agree that specific word instruction is important for academic as well as social success. Graves (1986) asserts that students who only partially understand words they read or hear often cannot fully comprehend what is being read or said. Furthermore, students with deficiencies in word knowledge often do not have the confidence to use partially understood words when they speak or write.

For your youngest students, instruction must be explicit, developmentally appropriate, and productive. Productivity often comes through engaging students with visuals and hands-on experiences as described in this activity.

In advance, gather or make several vocabulary cards with a picture on one side and a matching word on the other. Gather or make cards for a variety of categories such as colors, numbers, living and nonliving things, shapes, different types of transportation, musical instruments, and so on.

bicycle

car

Instructional Sequence

1. Advance Organizer

Tell students:

Get ready to learn more about words! When we listen to or read words, it is important to think. We need to think about what the words mean, and we need to think about how their meanings are like the meanings of other words.

One way to think about word meaning is to sort words into two groups. Boys, please stand on one side of the classroom. Girls, please stand on the other side. You have just sorted yourselves into two groups—boys and girls. Today we are going to sort pictures and words.

Here's how we will do it. I will show you a pile of vocabulary cards. Together we must sort the cards into two groups based on the word meanings. After the lesson, I will look to see if you understand these words when I say them and if you use these words when you speak or write.

2. Scaffolded Instruction

Model

Gather a pile of cards that clearly fall into the categories of colors and numbers. Play with the picture side of the cards first. Place one color card on the floor to the left and one number card on the floor to the right. Say: *This card shows the color **red**. This card shows the number **3**. Let's sort these pictures into colors and numbers.* Model how to sort the cards. Then say: *All the pictures on the left show colors. All the pictures on the right show numbers. Now we will play with words. When we are done, all the words on the left will be color words, and all the words on the right will be number words.*

Turn over the cards so the word sides are showing. Shuffle the cards. Repeat the activity using the words. Think aloud as you decide where to place each card. When you're done, lift the cards to look at the pictures and check your answers.

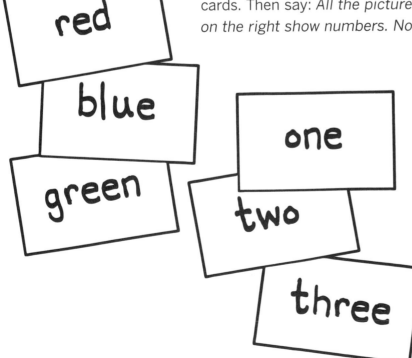

Do It With Me

Keep the color cards but choose a new card category to replace numbers, such as musical instruments. Work together to sort the cards, first by picture and then by word.

On Your Own

Keep the new card category and replace the color cards with the number cards. Circulate around the room as students sort the cards. Provide assistance as needed.

 ## 3. Ongoing Practice

As you introduce new words throughout the year, create or gather picture/word cards. Work with students to play "Picture/Word Sort" in the reading center. After students have played with one category of words several times, invite them to use the cards as flashcards and read the words aloud to you.

Say It-Write It Sequence

Grade Levels
2–3

Objective
Students will repeat multisyllabic words, break them into syllables, and identify spelling patterns.

 Big Idea

Background Information
Critical listening skills are key for effective learning in all content areas, especially in speaking, reading, and writing. The lack of critical listening ability especially affects vocabulary and sound-symbol correlation, or spelling. To know a word, students must be able to recognize its phonemic features, including the letters and sounds within each syllable. Often, students with poor vocabulary abilities cannot correctly say or repeat multisyllabic words. They have difficulty distinguishing and ordering syllables and the sounds within the syllables. Some students even have difficulty saying all the sounds in words containing consonant blends or clusters.

Phonemic Awareness

The National Reading Panel (2000) found that phonemic awareness is critical to reading success. Not only does awareness of the internal sound structure of words contribute to basic decoding ability, it also affects vocabulary. Knowing what a word means is understanding not only its definition and connotation, but also its phonological form and spelling patterns. In a recent reading study, researchers found that when capable readers encounter unknown written words, they translate the word into its spoken components as they attempt to decode and understand it. Therefore, if a student does not recognize the spoken components of the word, he or she will not comprehend the word.

During vocabulary instruction, it is important to call attention to the spoken components of words, specifically syllables, individual sounds, and spelling patterns. Helping students say a word correctly is one of the first steps to helping them improve their vocabulary. Helping students order the syllables and sounds will also help them to spell the word correctly. Both phonological form and orthographic form help students internalize words and improve vocabulary.

Say It-Write It Introduction

To begin the "Say It-Write It Sequence," choose a vocabulary word to introduce based on your advance lesson planning. Go through all the steps of the "Say It-Write It Sequence" for each new vocabulary word. This gives students many practice opportunities.

All students need practice repeating new words as syllables and writing the words. Through repeated multisensory practice, students learn the auditory and written properties of vocabulary words. This multisensory practice will help them remember words and recognize them in print.

Once you and the students become familiar with the "Say It-Write It" steps, the entire routine should take less than one minute. The routine is well worth the effort as students become critical listeners and learn a strategy for managing multisyllabic words.

out-stand-ing

Instructional Sequence

 ## 1. Advance Organizer

Tell students:

Get ready for a new vocabulary skill! Whenever we learn a new, unfamiliar, or difficult word, we must first pay attention to syllables and individual sounds within the syllables. Knowing syllables and sounds will help you remember the word. Many words sound similar with only a few sounds that are different. Paying attention to the syllables and the sounds in the syllables will help you learn to read and spell words, too.

We are going to practice working with difficult vocabulary words. Here's how we will do it. I will introduce a vocabulary word in two ways. First, you will say the word syllable by syllable. Then, you will write the word syllable by syllable. After the lesson, I will look to see if you can read, write, and say the word correctly.

2. Scaffolded Instruction

Model the Say-It Sequence

Follow these steps to introduce the vocabulary word you have chosen. Explain what a syllable is. Provide an example of how to identify a syllable. Model the "Say-It Sequence." Say the vocabulary word you are introducing. Say the word syllable by syllable while clapping.

Modeling Example *A syllable is the part of a word that has one vowel sound. It is the beat in a word. For example, the word* **dog** *has one syllable.* **Dog** *has one vowel sound and one beat, so it gets one clap. (Say and clap the word dog.)*

The word **wonderful** *has three vowel sounds. Listen while I clap out the word* **wonderful.** **Won** *(clap),* **der** *(clap),* **ful** *(clap).*

Do It With Me

Once you model the "Say-It Sequence," have students work with you. Say the word in unison. Then say the word alone and say and clap each syllable. Have students repeat the word and clap after you.

978-1-4129-5822-6

Model the Write-It Sequence

Follow these steps to introduce the vocabulary word you have chosen using the "Write-It Sequence." Say the word. Draw one scoop (or half circle) for each syllable, leaving enough room for letters to be written inside each scoop. Say each syllable as you write it inside each scoop. Call attention to any orthographic patterns.

Modeling Example *Let's keep working with* **wonderful**. *I will make a scoop each time I say a syllable in* **wonderful**. **Won** *(make a scoop),* **der** *(make a scoop),* **ful** *(make a scoop). I will touch each scoop, say the syllable, and write the letters.*

Do It With Me

Say the word. Have students repeat it. Guide students to use dry-erase boards to write one scoop for each syllable, leaving enough room for letters to be written inside each scoop. Say each syllable as you write it inside each scoop. Have students repeat after you.

On Your Own

Ask students to erase the syllables and then repeat the "Write-It Sequence" independently. Tour the room and provide redirection as needed.

3. Ongoing Practice

You can use the "Say It-Write It Sequence" whenever you introduce a new vocabulary word throughout the school year.

Public Record

Grade Levels
2–3

Objective
Students will record and graph vocabulary words.

 **Big Idea**

Background Information
A basic principle of effective vocabulary instruction is to establish word meaning by providing extensive multisensory exposure to a word in multiple contexts. Researchers have determined that 12 encounters with a word are necessary to place the word firmly in a student's lexicon.

Public Records
In the hustle of daily classroom activity, keeping track of how often words are used can be a challenge. To remedy this, you can keep a Public Record that is visible to all students and holds everyone accountable for the words.

If you do not use the "Let's Listen and Learn" banner to record vocabulary words (pages 24–27), you can make a Public Record. To do this, use chart paper and markers to create a graph like the example below. Write the words in the left column. Each time a word is used, check off the box next to the word. Just by glancing at the chart, it will become apparent which words have been used often and which words need additional practice.

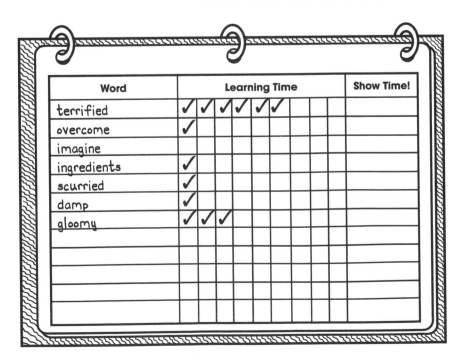

Word	Learning Time									Show Time!
terrified	✓	✓	✓	✓	✓	✓				
overcome	✓									
imagine										
ingredients	✓									
scurried	✓									
damp	✓									
gloomy	✓	✓	✓							

Instructional Sequence

1. Advance Organizer

Tell students:

In order to remember new vocabulary words, adults and children alike must practice and use a word at least 12 times. In addition to using the dictionary and writing meanings in your Vocabulary Logs, we are going to keep track of vocabulary words. Today we are going to post a graph called a Public Record. Each time I introduce a new word, I am going to write it on this graph. Each time we use the word in a class activity, we will check off a box next to the word.

Our Public Record is a bar graph. You may have used bar graphs in math. Tell a partner when you have used a bar graph and the advantages of using the graph. Who would like to share their ideas with the class?

I expect you to pay attention and remind me when to check off a box next to a word. I will not remind you about any of the words. That's your job! When we have used the word 12 times, you will be expected to know that word. I should be able to give you a test on that word, and you should be able to tell the meaning of the word, use the word in a sentence, give an antonym or synonym, and even make an analogy using that word. I will not expect you to know a word until there are 12 boxes checked. After the twelfth box is checked, it's show time!

2. Scaffolded Instruction

Model

Post a Public Record chart that you have made. Record two or three vocabulary words that you chose based on your advance lesson planning. Go through each word, thinking aloud and describing what you will do as students encounter these words in your explicit vocabulary lessons and content-area lessons.

Do It With Me

Choose one word and complete the "Say It-Write It Sequence" (pages 42–45). Invite a student to check off one box on the Public Record to show that the class has been exposed to the word.

3. Ongoing Practice

Throughout subsequent school days, invite students to remind you when to check off boxes on the graph.

Keyword Fun

Materials
• drawing paper

Grade Levels
K–3

Objective
Students will use a mnemonic device to remember word meanings.

 Big Idea

Background Information
The keyword method is a two-stage mnemonic technique in which a student develops understanding of a new vocabulary word by making an acoustic link (developing a keyword related to the word) and an imagery link (forming an image associated with the word). For example, if the new word is *stable*, meaning "a building in which livestock are kept," the keyword could be *stay*. You could then generate a mental image of a horse staying behind a stable door. Logical or silly images can be generated to help students absorb and remember the meaning of the word. This technique was originally used for learning foreign languages, but it has since been applied to classroom vocabulary instruction.

Instructional Sequence

1. Advance Organizer

Tell students:

When you learn a new word, it is important to understand what it means and how it is used. When you truly understand a word, you can begin to read it, write it, and use it in your everyday speech. Today we are going to do a fun activity to help us remember new words and their meanings.

Think about times when you have seen funny pictures. Where did you see them? We are going to use pictures and words we already know to learn new words. The game we will play is called "Keyword Fun." After today, we will use the game from time to time when we learn new words. Once we learn the words and play the game, I will expect that you know the meanings of the new words, and I will watch for correct usage when you talk to me.

2. Scaffolded Instruction

Model

Follow these steps to introduce "Keyword Fun."

Introduce the word and tell its meaning. On the board, write a vocabulary word that you have chosen in your advance lesson planning. For example, you might use the word *hiccups*. Give a KFD (Kid-Friendly Definition) for the word (pages 11–18.) For example, you might define *hiccups* as "an uncontrollable gasp that makes a funny sound in your throat."

Name a keyword for the vocabulary word. Tell students that a keyword is a reminder for the new word. It should be a word that they already know, it should sound like an important part of the new word, and it should be easy to picture in their mind. For *hiccups*, you might use the keyword *cup*. If the keyword is part of the vocabulary word, underline it on the board (i.e., *hic<u>cup</u>s*).

Make a visual link between the keyword and the vocabulary word. Show students how to make a visual link between the keyword and the vocabulary word. For example, for *hiccups* and *cup* you might say: *I'm picturing myself drinking a cup of water as I get the hiccups. The water sprays everywhere! Everyone, try to picture the same thing.*

Remind children of the meaning of the vocabulary word. Tell students that the next time you see the new word, you will picture that image. For example, the next time you see the word *hiccups*, you will picture yourself drinking from a cup and hiccupping.

Do It With Me

Choose a vocabulary word from those you have planned to teach. Follow the modeling steps to have students work with you to create a keyword and image.

 3. Ongoing Practice

Repeat this activity several times during the school year with new vocabulary words. Always model or work together with younger students. Older students can sometimes work with partners or on their own to create keyword images. Invite these students to share their ideas. Once students have demonstrated proficiency with the process, invite them to illustrate their keyword images and write the new vocabulary words under the pictures.

ranch
keyword: ran

978-1-4129-5822-6

Think, Pair, Share

Grade Levels
2–3

Materials
• none

Objective
Students will process word meanings and create their own connections.

 ## Big Idea

Background Information
Research consistently indicates that learners understand and remember vocabulary better when they elaborate through speaking and writing. Having students generate their own word examples gives them the opportunity to connect words to their own lives. Being able to talk about ideas first with a partner, and then with the whole class, provides opportunities to interact with words as well as with classmates. Students must actively listen to each other and later make judgments about word usage—all keys to internalizing new vocabulary.

Instructional Sequence

 ## 1. Advance Organizer
Tell students:

To remember new words, you need practice in reading, writing, speaking, and listening to them. Today we are going to play a game called "Think, Pair, Share." You will work with a partner to talk about a new vocabulary word that I have chosen for you.

Let's form partners. Now, tell your partner about a time when you have seen someone make a list. Was it a shopping list? Was it a batting list for a baseball team? Today you will brainstorm alone and then share ideas with a partner. We're going to have fun. I expect you to think quietly alone first and then listen carefully when you hear your partner's ideas. After today, I will listen for you to use the new word in your speaking and watch for it in your writing.

 ## 2. Scaffolded Instruction

Model
Say a vocabulary word that you chose based on your advance lesson planning. Choose a student to help you model. Think aloud as you complete these steps:

Think Take one minute to think about examples of the word in real life.

Pair Work with a student volunteer for 90 seconds. Together, think of new examples and take turns saying them. At the end of the 90 seconds, choose your favorite example.

Share Have the student volunteer share the example with the class. Explain that each pair will get to share with the class.

Do It With Me
Choose a new vocabulary word. Have student pairs work with you to play the game, following the steps you described and demonstrated during modeling.

 ## 3. Ongoing Practice
Repeat this activity several times during the school year with a variety of student pairings.

Introduce Synonyms

Grade Levels
K–3

Objective
Students will study synonyms to establish and build on meanings of vocabulary words.

 ## Big Idea

Background Information
As students become more skilled in comprehending word meanings, they can begin to work with categories of words, such as synonyms. Before applying the term *synonym* to new vocabulary, firmly establish the concept of *similar*, the meaning of the term *synonym*, and the variations in word meanings that are acceptable in each category.

    For this lesson, ask second and third graders to record synonyms in their Vocabulary Logs (page 38).

Instructional Sequence

 ### 1. Advance Organizer
Tell students:

*One good way to learn new words is to think about how the meaning of a new word is like the meaning of other words. A **synonym** is a word that has the same or almost the same meaning as another word. **Sssssynonym** means **sssssame**.*

    *Say the word **synonym** with me. **Synonym** has three syllables. I will clap the syllables for you: **syn** (clap), **o** (clap), **nym** (clap). Repeat the word after me and clap it out.*

    We will work with synonyms throughout the year. Once we have a lot of practice, I will expect you to identify synonyms when you read, write, and speak.

• pairs of magazine pictures of the following: dog/pup, friend/pal, car/auto
• pairs of synonym picture/word index cards (1 card per student)
• permanent marker

Materials

cup   mug

2. Scaffolded Instruction

Model

Hold up a magazine picture of a dog. Write the word *dog* across the picture in permanent marker. Say: *dog*. Hold up another magazine picture of a dog. Write the word *pup* across the picture in permanent marker. Say: *pup*. Explain: *The words **dog** and **pup** are synonyms. They mean almost the same thing. Let's look at some other synonyms.* Repeat with other magazine pictures that represent these words: *friend/pal, car/auto*.

Do It With Me

Hold up the following classroom objects, and invite students to brainstorm with you synonyms for them: *book (paperback), watch (clock), light (lamp), curtain (drape), shade (blind)*. Second and third graders can record the words on dry-erase boards or in their Vocabulary Logs (page 38).

 ## 3. Ongoing Practice

Distribute a synonym picture/word card to each student. Have students seek their synonym match. When all students have found their match, ask them to read aloud their cards for verification.

dog

pup

978-1-4129-5822-6

Rename the Story

Grade Levels
K–3

Objective
Students will apply knowledge of synonyms to expand their understanding of vocabulary words.

 ## Big Idea

Background Information
Once students have been introduced to synonyms, have them apply their knowledge to new vocabulary. "Rename the Story" is a valuable game that can help students expand their vocabularies so they can transfer it to reading, writing, and speaking. Be sure to modify the lesson for different grade levels as described.

Instructional Sequence

 ### 1. Advance Organizer
Tell students:

Now that you have been introduced to synonyms, we are going to use them to learn new words. It's important to learn new words so we can be better readers, writers, speakers, and listeners.

After we learn some new words today, I will expect you to be able to use the new words when you read, write, or speak. Watch out; these words might even show up on a test!

2. Scaffolded Instruction

Model
Show the cover of a version of *Little Red Riding Hood.* Track the print as you read aloud the story. After reading, say: *Let's use synonyms to rename this story. We will take each important word, one at a time, and make up a new title.* Think aloud as you provide a synonym for each important word in the title. Explain how you chose each word. For example, you might rename the story *Small Crimson Cape.*

Do It With Me

Choose a familiar picture book whose title is easy to rename using synonyms. (Students should have some experience with the storyline.) Work together with students to rename the story using synonyms.

On Your Own

Provide each student with a picture book to review and perhaps read independently. Ask him or her to think of synonyms to rename the story. Provide assistance as necessary. Then give students a sheet of drawing paper. Ask them to illustrate a scene from the story and label the picture with the original and new title. Second- and third-grade students can record new synonyms in their Vocabulary Logs (page 38).

The Three Little Pigs   The Trio of Small Swine

Introduce Antonyms

Grade Levels
K–3

Objective
Students will study antonyms to establish and build on the meanings of vocabulary words.

 ## Big Idea

Background Information
Once student have worked with synonyms, they can begin to work with antonyms. While identifying opposites is a common skill explored in the early grades, students need to understand that words are associated with this concept, and these words are called *antonyms*. Before applying the term *antonym* to new vocabulary, firmly establish the concept of *opposite*, the meaning of the term *antonym,* and the variations in word meanings that are acceptable in each category.

For this lesson, ask second and third graders to record antonyms in their Vocabulary Logs (page 38).

Materials
- pairs of magazine pictures that represent the following: run/walk, friend/enemy, wet/dry
- pairs of antonym picture/word index cards (1 card per student)
- permanent marker

Instructional Sequence

1. Advance Organizer
Tell students:

One good way to learn new words is to think about how the meaning of a new word is different from the meanings of other words. An **antonym** *is a word that has the opposite meaning or almost the opposite of another word.*

Say the word **antonym** *with me.* **Antonym** *has three syllables. I will clap the syllables for you:* **ant** *(clap),* **o** *(clap),* **nym** *(clap). Repeat the word after me as you clap it out.*

We will work with antonyms throughout the year. Once we have had a lot of practice, I will expect you to identify antonyms when you read, write, and speak.

young   old

2. Scaffolded Instruction

Model

Hold up a magazine picture that represents the word *fast*. Write the word *fast* across the picture in permanent marker. Say: *fast*. Hold up another magazine picture that represents the word *slow*. Write the word *slow* across the picture in permanent marker. Say: *slow*. Explain: *The words **fast** and **slow** are antonyms. They mean the opposite of one another. Let's look at some other antonyms.* Repeat with other magazine pictures that represent these words: *friend/enemy, wet/dry*.

Do It With Me

Role-play and name the following actions and guide students to brainstorm antonyms for them: *sleep (wake up), sad (happy), cry (laugh), quiet (loud), teacher (student)*. Second and third graders can record the words on dry-erase boards or in their Vocabulary Logs (page 38).

 ## 3. Ongoing Practice

Distribute an antonym picture/word card to each student. Have students seek their antonym match. When all students have found their match, ask them to read aloud their cards for verification.

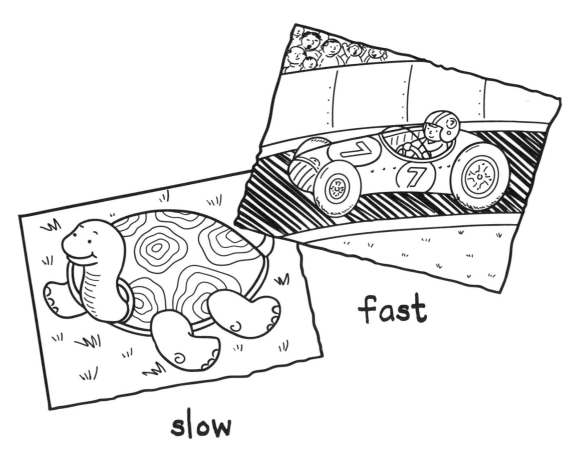

fast

slow

978-1-4129-5822-6

Antonym Memory Game

Grade Levels
2–3

Objective
Students will understand antonyms and their meanings.

 Big Idea

Background Information
After introducing students to antonyms, place antonym word cards in the reading center and invite pairs of students to play the following game. Be sure to switch out cards as students show knowledge of them through reading, writing, speaking, and listening comprehension.

Instructional Sequence

1. Advance Organizer
Tell students:

You know that you need to work with antonyms to learn new words and be better readers, writers, speakers, and listeners. You have worked with antonyms before. Today you will play a game with them.

How many of you have played a memory match game? When did you play it? With whom? Today you will play the game with antonyms. Don't worry if you don't know how. I will teach you how to play.

Your goal in playing the game is to find antonym word pairs. After you play the game, I will watch to see if you can use the new words in your reading, speaking, and writing.

978-1-4129-5822-6

2. Scaffolded Instruction

Model

Place the 12 antonym word cards facedown in random order on a table in a three-by-four grid. Turn over two cards. Read aloud the words on the cards. Think aloud as you decide if the words are antonyms. If they are, keep the cards. If they are not antonyms, turn the cards back over and keep trying until you make a match.

Do It With Me

Play the rest of the game as individual students take turns with your guidance. Finish the game with students taking one turn each.

On Your Own

Place the cards in the reading center. Invite pairs of students to visit the center and play the game.

 ## 3. Ongoing Practice

Change out the antonym word card pairs throughout the year, and invite students to play the "Antonym Memory Game" in the reading center.

CHAPTER 3

Strategy Lessons

Use Picture Clues

Grade Levels
K–1

Objective
Students will use picture clues to learn new vocabulary.

 **Big Idea**

Background Information
Young learners often encounter new vocabulary during picture book reading. When a student hears or reads a new word, he or she needs strategies to make meaning from the word. Skilled, fluent readers have the ability to recognize when they have a problem with word meaning and use decoding and comprehension strategies to correct it. At-risk or very young learners need explicit instruction in order to become skilled in gleaning vocabulary information.

One way young learners can determine the meaning of new vocabulary is to consider picture clues. With a few simple steps, these students can become more aware of supportive illustrations and gain valuable vocabulary skills.

Instructional Sequence

 1. Advance Organizer

Tell students:

Today you will learn a way to find the meanings of new words that you hear or see in picture books.

Let's begin. Point to your eyes. What do you use your eyes for? That's right. You use your eyes to see things. You can learn a lot about new words just by using your eyes. Sometimes when you hear or read a new word, you can look at the pictures in picture books for clues to help you learn the word. Today we are going to learn how to do this.

After today, I will watch to see if you look at pictures to help you figure out new words. Let's get started.

Materials
- Picture Clues reproducibles
- transparencies of Picture Clues reproducibles
- simple picture books with supportive illustrations

2. Scaffolded Instruction

Model
Give students copies of the **Picture Clues reproducibles (pages 63–64)**. Display a transparency of the first reproducible. Model how to use picture clues to learn new vocabulary. Begin with Picture 1.

Modeling Example *Let's pretend that I am reading this sentence in a picture book:* **The puppy plays . . .** *I stop at the underlined word and think, "I don't know this word. What can I do?" The first thing I do is look at the first letter of the word,* **/t/**, **t**. *Then I look at the picture. I ask myself, "What is the dog playing that starts with* **t**? *I know! The dog is playing tug-of-war!" So, this sentence must say:* **The puppy plays tug-of-war**.

Do It With Me
Follow the modeling example to work with students to learn the new vocabulary example for Picture 2: *The cap was on a <u>branch</u>.* Have student volunteers help you discover the new word.

On Your Own
Ask students to work with a partner and think aloud to learn the new vocabulary examples in Pictures 3–8. Discuss how students used picture clues after they discovered the words.

 ## 3. Ongoing Practice
Repeat this activity several times during the school year with new vocabulary words as you read aloud picture books or when students read independently. For the first few vocabulary words, model the process before having students practice the strategy on their own.

The cat naps on the rug.

The bunny bounces a ball.

Name _____   Date _____

Picture Clues

1. The puppy plays <u>tug-of-war</u>.

2. The cap was on a <u>branch</u>.

3. The baby rode in a <u>buggy</u>.

4. The man took our <u>order</u>.

Picture Clues

5. The cat <u>naps</u> on the rug.

6. The bunny <u>bounces</u> a ball.

7. Tim read a book about the <u>ocean</u>.

8. The race car <u>sped</u> around the track.

Use Context for Meaning

Grade Levels
2–3

Objective
Students will learn the steps of using context to determine the meaning of unknown vocabulary words.

 Big Idea

Materials
- various literature excerpts on overhead transparencies
- teacher-made Steps for Using Context Clues poster
- vocabulary logs
- fiction and nonfiction student books

Background Information
When helping students use context to determine word meaning, be sure to work with text that is at their "just right" level. "Just right" text is essential because before students can be expected to use context to determine the meaning of unknown words, they must be able to decode and understand at least 90% of the words in a passage, recognize which words they do not understand, and comprehend the majority of the passage.

Keep in mind that teaching context to determine word meaning should not be the primary focus of vocabulary instruction. Reading researchers agree that solely relying on context to improve vocabulary is often not enough. (Feldman & Kinsella, 2002; Santa, Havens, & Valdes, 2004). Use other vocabulary strategies in conjunction with context.

Instructional Sequence

1. Advance Organizer
Tell students:

Sometimes when you are reading, you will come to a word that you do not know. You may be able to use the words and sentences around that word to figure out what it means. When you use the other words and sentences around the word to determine its meaning, that is called learning from the context. "Using context clues" refers to reading other words and sentences to figure out a word.

You need to learn to use context clues because they will help you better understand what you are reading. You have been writing words in a Vocabulary Log. Now you will learn to use context to figure out the meaning of those words.

Be sure to have your Vocabulary Log and reading book ready. First, I will show you the steps in using context clues. Next, we will practice, and then you will use your own books and words to practice using context. I will expect you to know and demonstrate the steps when you come to an unknown word.

2. Scaffolded Instruction

Model

Display a Steps for Using Context Clues poster that you made in advance and a transparency of a text excerpt with a complex vocabulary word. Model the steps of using context to determine the meaning of an unknown word. Refer to the poster as you work.

Steps for Using Context Clues

1. Underline the unfamiliar word.

2. Read the sentences before and after the word.

3. Describe what you know so far.

4. Summarize what the story is about to this point.

5. Use what you know about the story and the sentence to guess what the word might mean.

6. Read the sentence again and substitute your idea of the word.

7. Decide if the word makes sense.

978-1-4129-5822-6

Modeling Example *This example is an excerpt from Marvin Redpost: Is He a Girl?* by Louis Sachar. *The selection from the text is:* **He dreamed he was hanging from the monkey bars by his knees. A warm breeze blew in his face. Birds were singing.**

I can read the word **breeze**, *but I do not understand what it means. I do not understand what is blowing in his face. I will underline* **breeze**.

Now I have to read the sentences around that word and think about what they mean. **He dreamed he was hanging from the monkey bars by his knees. Birds were singing.** *Now I will describe what I know so far. I need to put this in my own words. I know he must be outside since he is hanging from the monkey bars. If the birds are singing, it must be a nice day.*

Now I will summarize and explain what the story is about to this point. At this point in the story, the main character is worried that he might be turning into a girl. He is dreaming about "girl things" while hanging from the monkey bars.

I'm going to guess what the word might mean. Maybe the word **breeze** *means "a light wind." When I'm outside on a playground, the only thing that blows in my face is the wind. Let's try it:* **A warm, light wind blew in his face.** *That makes perfect sense!* **Breeze** *must mean "a light wind."*

Do It With Me

Have students help you go through the steps again with a different excerpt as you refer to the poster. You may want to use several excerpts, including those from students' current studies.

On Your Own

During the same session, have students work independently with partners. Have pairs choose a word from their Vocabulary Logs and work together to go through the steps. Walk around the room, providing assistance as needed.

 ## 3. Ongoing Practice

Once students are comfortable, you may want to add this activity to their Vocabulary Log time. Start by having students work with one word a week. Gradually work up to all five words, perhaps as a written homework assignment.

Compound Words

Materials
• sentence strips

Grade Levels
2–3

Objective
Students will identify compound words and their meanings.

 **Big Idea**

Background Information
A compound word is a combination of two or more words that function as a single unit of meaning. Compound words can be written as a single word such as *toothpaste,* a hyphenated word such as *merry-go-round,* or two or more separate words such as *book report.* This lesson focuses on compound words written as single words.

Young or at-risk learners can benefit from strategies that help them identify and understand compound words. The following activity helps students predict word meaning by studying compound word parts.

In advance, choose two or three compound words as vocabulary words. Use the "Word Selection and Definition" strategy (pages 11–18) to help you determine appropriate words, or see page 70 for a possible word list.

butterfly

Instructional Sequence

1. Advance Organizer
Tell students:

Some vocabulary words that you read or listen to are made up of two smaller words. These words are called **compound words***. Listen to this definition:* **A compound word is a combination of two or more words that together make a word with a single meaning.**

Listen as I say this word: **homework***. Raise your hand if you have ever had homework.* **Homework** *is a compound word. Listen to the parts:* **home***,* **work***. If I think about the meaning of the parts, I can figure out what* **homework** *means.* **Homework** *means work that you do at home.*

Once you have studied the compound words that we learn today, I will look for correct usage in your everyday reading, writing, and speaking. When I say the new words, I will expect you to understand what I am saying.

2. Scaffolded Instruction

Model

In advance, choose a compound word from your lesson planning. Write the word on the board in a sentence, and model how to predict its meaning from the two parts. For example, you might write this sentence on the board: *Pam wore her raincoat.*

Modeling Example *If I were reading this sentence and I couldn't figure out the last word, I could do this. First, I look at the word to see if it is made up of two smaller words that can each stand alone. Good news—it is! This word is made up of the smaller words* **rain** *and* **coat***. Knowing the meaning of each word in a compound word can help me figure out the meaning of the whole word. So, let's think about the meaning of each smaller word. I know what* **rain** *is, and I know what a* **coat** *is. How might these words work together to create a new meaning? I know! A* **raincoat** *must be a coat that you wear in the rain.*

Pam wore her raincoat.

Do It With Me

Choose a new compound word and write it on the board in a sentence. Do not underline the compound word. First, have students help you identify the compound word. Then, work together with students to predict its meaning, thinking aloud about the meaning of each individual word.

On Your Own

Ahead of time, prepare a sentence strip for each pair of students. Write a sentence on each strip that contains a compound vocabulary word. Organize students into pairs. Give each pair a sentence strip. Ask students to find the compound word, underline it, and determine its meaning. Have pairs read aloud their sentence and explain their findings.

3. Ongoing Practice

Repeat this activity throughout the year as students encounter compound words in their reading or as you read aloud to them. Following is a list of possible compound words:

afternoon	grasshopper	popcorn
airport	homemade	seaside
backache	hometown	snowflake
backspace	horseback	sunflower
baseball	jellyfish	superhero
bookcase	keyboard	supermarket
butterfly	keyhole	textbook
crosswalk	lifeboat	toothbrush
doghouse	lifetime	underarm
fireworks	necktie	upstairs
footprint	nobody	weekend
grandmother	noisemaker	windowsill

afternoon

butterfly

doghouse

sunflower

footprint

baseball

grasshopper

978-1-4129-5822-6

Multiple-Meaning Mimes

Grade Levels
K–1

Objective
Students will explore words with multiple meanings.

 **Big Idea**

Background Information
The English language is filled with words that have more than one meaning. Homonyms, homophones, and homographs are categories of words that have multiple meanings. *Homonyms* are words that have the same spelling and pronunciation but have different meanings and origins. For example, *can* is a homonym because it can mean "to have the ability to" and "a metal vessel." *Homophones* are words that have the same pronunciation but have different spellings and meanings, such as *air* and *heir*. *Homographs* are words that are spelled the same but are usually different in meaning or pronunciation, such as *wind*, which can mean "blowing air" and "to encircle with loops or layers."

Beginning readers and English language learners in particular need practice with multiple-meaning words because context often provides the best clues for pronunciation and/or meaning. This lesson on homonyms focuses on word meaning only rather than word meaning in combination with pronunciation and spelling.

Instructional Sequence

1. Advance Organizer
Tell students:

Words can be tricky. Sometimes a word can mean more than one thing, even when the word is spelled the same and pronounced in the same way. Listen to these sentences. Which words are the same? **I am going to <u>train</u> my dog. Mark rode on the <u>train</u>.**

What did the word **train** *mean in the first sentence? Tell a friend about a time when you saw someone try to train an animal. What did the word* **train** *mean in the second sentence? Tell a friend about a time when you saw or rode on a train.*

Today we are going to work with words that have the same spelling and pronunciation but have different meanings. It is going to be a lot of

Materials
- construction paper
- drawing paper
- crayons or markers

bat

fun. After we study the words, I want you to listen for them in school and at home and be ready to learn to read and write them.

2. Scaffolded Instruction

Model

Write the word *coat* on the board. Read the word aloud. Say this sentence: *I put on my <u>coat</u>.* Pantomime putting on your coat. Then say this sentence: *I am painting this chair with a red <u>coat</u> of paint.* Pantomime painting the chair.

Tell students: *The word* **coat** *is a homonym. It is a word that has more than one meaning. When I listen to or read sentences, I have to listen carefully because some words have more than one meaning. I have to listen and decide what these words mean.*

Do It With Me

Write the word *duck* on the board. Read aloud the word and say: *The brown <u>duck</u> waddled down the road.* Invite students to pantomime waddling like a duck as you waddle with them. Then say: *<u>Duck</u>! Here comes a baseball!* Pantomime ducking from a ball, and invite students to duck with you.

On Your Own

Write the word *punch* on the board. Read aloud the word and say: *I drank fruit <u>punch</u> at the party.* Challenge students to pantomime the word *punch* as it appears in the sentence. Then say: *Marco likes to <u>punch</u> the punching bag.* Invite students to pantomime this sentence as well.

Tell students: *Now we are going to practice using these words in sentences to show we know the meaning. We are going to draw and have some fun.*

Give students drawing paper and have them draw pictures to illustrate two different meanings for the word *punch*. Have them write sentences to go with the illustrations.

coat

978-1-4129-5822-6

📖 3. Ongoing Practice

Form four groups of students. Provide each group with one of the following sentences that you have written on construction paper:

- The mother <u>duck</u> led her fuzzy ducklings around the pond.

- Mary had to <u>duck</u> so the ball would not hit her.

- Jake overfilled his glass with <u>punch</u>, and it spilled all over the table.

- *The toy robot used its right arm to <u>punch</u> the other robot.*

Guide each group to illustrate their sentence. Challenge groups to tour the room and find another group with a matching underlined word in their sentence. Glue the pairs of *duck* and *punch* pictures back-to-back and use string to hang them around the classroom.

Repeat the activity throughout the year with homonyms that you have chosen during lesson planning. These words might include: *watch, park, alarm, bill, bit, beam, blue, calf, cape, cold, dress, fast, fly, fork, rock,* and *ruler.*

The mother <u>duck</u> led her fuzzy ducklings around the pond.

Mary had to <u>duck</u> so the ball would not hit her.

Multiple-Meaning Pictures

Materials
• Homophones Flashcards reproducible
• dry-erase boards
• drawing paper
• crayons or markers

Grade Levels
2–3

Objective
Students will explore words with multiple meanings.

Big Idea

Background Information
Words that have more than one meaning are common in the English language. Homonyms, homophones, and homographs are all categories of multiple-meaning words. *Homophones* are words that have the same pronunciation but have different spellings and meanings, such as *air* and *heir*. This lesson focuses on homophones and invites students to explore word meaning and spelling. See "Multiple-Meaning Mimes" (pages 71–73) for a lesson on homonyms.

Beginning readers and English language learners in particular need practice with multiple-meaning words because context often provides the best clues for pronunciation and meaning.

meet   meat

Instructional Sequence

→ 1. Advance Organizer

Tell students:

The English language is full of interesting words. Sometimes words can sound the same but have totally different spellings and meanings. Listen to these sentences. Which words sound the same? Would you like to meet *my sister? Be sure to eat your* meat *before you have dessert.*

What did the word **meet** *mean in the first sentence? Tell a friend about a time when you were nervous to meet someone. What did the word* **meat** *mean in the second sentence? Tell a friend about a time when you ate meat that tasted very good.*

Today we are going to work with words that have different spellings and meanings but sound the same. It's going to be a lot of fun. After we study the words, I want you to listen for them in school and at home and be ready to read and write them.

hair   hare

⊞ 2. Scaffolded Instruction

Model

Write the following sentence on the board and underline the word *hair:* *Henry never combs his* hair. Read aloud the sentence. Then write and read aloud this sentence, underlining the word *hare: The fuzzy brown* hare *jumped out of the cabbage patch.*

Say: *The words* **hair** *and* **hare** *are homophones. They sound the same but are spelled differently and have different meanings. When I listen to sentences, I have to listen carefully because some words have more than one meaning. I have to listen and decide what these words mean. If I were to read the sentences, I would look at the words around the multiple-meaning words as well as the pictures to find out what the words mean.*

Do It With Me

Write the following sentence on the board: *The green knight won the joust.* Have students copy the sentence on dry-erase boards. Read aloud the sentence. Then write and read aloud this sentence: *I ate popcorn last night.* Have students copy this sentence on dry-erase boards. Work with them to identify and underline the homophones *night* and *knight.*

Remind students: *Homophones are words that sound the same but are spelled differently and have different meanings. When you listen to sentences, you have to listen very carefully to help you decide what these special words mean. When you read sentences, you must study the words around new words and look at the pictures to find out what the new words mean.*

On Your Own

Write these words on the board: *mail, male.* Explain their meanings. Challenge students to work with a partner to write a sentence that uses each word. Invite volunteers to read their sentences aloud.

 ## 3. Ongoing Practice

Organize three groups of students. Provide each group with a set of homophone index cards: *hair/hare, knight/night, mail/male.* Have each group act out a sentence for each word.

Repeat the activity throughout the year with other homophones, such as those provided on the **Homophones Flashcards reproducible (page 77)**. Keep a running list, and invite students to add homophones from read-alouds or books they read on their own.

Homophones Flashcards

pail	pale
steal	steel
your	you're
tied	tide
threw	through
soar	sore
paws	pause
horse	hoarse

Prefixes and Suffixes

Materials

- Most Common Prefixes reproducible
- Most Common Suffixes reproducible
- different-colored index cards
- prefixes and suffixes posters
- overhead projector and transparencies

Grade Levels

2–3

Objective

Students will determine the meanings of words using common prefixes and suffixes.

 ## Big Idea

Background Information

Not all words can be explained from the words and sentences around them. Students also need to know how to use word parts, or morphemes, to figure out what a word means. A *morpheme* is the smallest part of a word that has meaning. Prefixes, suffixes, and word roots are morphemes.

Many struggling readers do not realize that words are made up of parts, nor do they know how prefixes and suffixes can affect the meanings of words. Directly teaching these word parts and how to locate them will do much to foster vocabulary growth and improve decoding ability.

Initial instruction should focus on morphemes that are clearly recognizable and easily translatable into a meaningful definition. More obscure and less common prefixes and suffixes should be taught after students have a firm grasp of the most frequently used morphemes.

Preparation

To prepare for the lesson, consult the **Most Common Prefixes** and **Most Common Suffixes reproducibles (pages 82–83)**. The morphemes are listed in order of frequency. The first five prefixes and suffixes should be taught first, followed by the other word parts in order. Alternate between groups using the reproducibles as a guide. Record the examples on two large posters and display them prominently in the classroom. You might also wish to reproduce the examples and provide them for students to use when reading.

In addition to the posters, write prefixes and suffixes on large index cards. On the front of each card, write the word part in large black letters. On the back of each card, write the meaning and at least ten examples of words containing this word part. Also provide a definition of two or three words. Be sure to use different words each time so students have an opportunity to hear and say a wide variety of words. For example, you might write *inactive = not active, invisible = not visible, invalid = not valid.*

Color-code the cards for additional cueing, using a different-colored index card for each of the two parts: prefixes and suffixes.

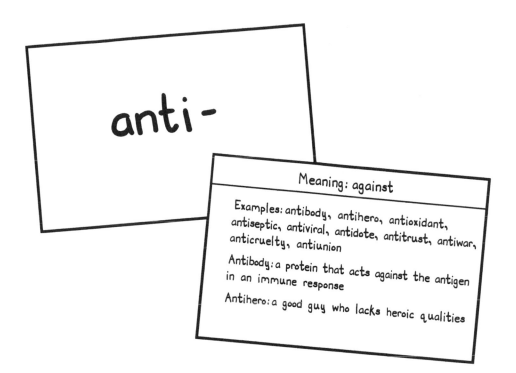

Instructional Sequence

 ### 1. Advance Organizer

Tell students:

We are going to learn about two word parts that add meaning to words. These parts are prefixes and suffixes. Learning about word parts can help you learn the meanings of new words. It will also improve your ability to read, write, and speak.

When you are reading and you come across a big word that you do not know, you can use the context to determine the meaning. But you may also be able to use word parts to break the word into smaller sections so you can determine what the word means.

*The wall charts I have displayed show word parts that you will learn over several lessons. We will go slowly through the word parts so you can learn them well. You will learn the meaning of each word part, and you will be able to identify the word parts when they appear in writing. Today we will work with the prefix **in-**. After all the word parts have been introduced, you will be able to determine the meaning of a word by breaking down the parts.*

 **2. Scaffolded Instruction**

Model

Explain to students that prefixes are word parts that appear at the beginning of words to modify the meaning. Point to the prefix *in-* on the Most Common Prefixes chart and read it aloud. Display the word card you made. (See Preparation, pages 78–79) Define this new morpheme. Show the morpheme card and say: *This word part is **in-**. Say it with me: **in-**.* Ask students to repeat the word part. Tell the meaning of the word part: ***In-** means "not."* Have students repeat the meaning of the word part. Ask: *What does **in-** mean?* Have students repeat the meaning of the morpheme.

Provide an oral example such as *incomplete*. Emphasize the word part as you say the word. For example: *Listen while I say a word containing the prefix **in-**, **incomplete**.* Have students repeat the word. Give the meaning of the word using the word and the meaning in a complete sentence: ***Incomplete** means "not complete."*

Then have students repeat the word and the meaning in a complete sentence. Ask: *What does **incomplete** mean?* Students respond: ***Incomplete** means "not complete."*

Say a sentence with *incomplete* using a situation relevant to the students: *Here is a sentence using that word: **Christina's homework was incomplete, so she did not get credit for it.*** Then ask students to volunteer sentences with the word *incomplete*. Repeat the activity with several additional words containing *in-*.

My homework is *incomplete* because I was sick.

Do It With Me

Have students write the word examples containing *in-* as you write them on the board. Say: *Here are the words we just practiced saying. Let's see what they look like in writing.* Have students work with you to circle the word part. Together, go through each word containing the newly introduced word part.

On Your Own

Have students brainstorm and write other words that have the prefix *in-*.

3. Ongoing Practice

Complete the Modeling, Do It With Me, and On Your Own strategies throughout the year with different prefixes and suffixes.

As you complete the lessons, add the newly learned morphemes to the card deck. (See Preparation, pages 78–79.) From time to time, go through the word part deck, showing one part at a time and having students repeat what they read.

You might also wish to create crossword puzzles or fill-in-the-blank worksheets that feature words containing previously learned word parts. Invite students to circle word parts and/or write the word meanings in the puzzles.

Prefix Review

Across
1. not complete
5. pay again
6. act between

Down
2. not able
3. view before
4. part away from

978-1-4129-5822-6

Most Common Prefixes

PREFIX	MEANING	EXAMPLES
in-	not	incorrect, inactive
un-	not, opposite of	unhappy, unlikely
dis-	not, opposite of	distrust, disappear
mis-	wrongly	misspell, misbehave
fore-	before	forefather, foreground
re-	again	rethink, rewrite
de-	down, away from	deplane, depart
pre-	before	pretest, precaution
en-, em-	cause to be	enable, embrace
non-	not	nonskid, nonfiction
in-, im-	in or into	input, inside
over-	too much	overeat, overpay
sub-	under	subway, submarine
inter-	between	interstate, interact
trans-	across	transatlantic, transport
super-	above	superhero, supersonic
semi-	half	semicircle, semiannual
anti-	against	antiwar, antibiotic
mid-	middle	midday, midyear
under-	too little, below	underpaid, underground

All other prefixes (approximately 100) account for only 3% of all the words containing prefixes.

Sources:

Blevins, W. (2001). *Teaching phonics and word study in the intermediate grades*. New York, NY: Scholastic.

Henry, M. (2003). *Unlocking literacy: Effective decoding and spelling instruction*. Baltimore, MD: Paul H. Brookes.

Yoshimoto, R. (1997). Phonemes, phonetics, and phonograms. *Teaching Exceptional Children, 29*(3), 43–47.

Most Common Suffixes

SUFFIX	MEANING	EXAMPLES
-s, -es	plural	cats, boxes
-ed	past-tense verbs	jumped, laughed
-ing	verbs, present participle	running, singing
-ly	characteristic of	sadly, quietly
-er, -or	one who, connected with	jogger, actor
-ion, -tion, -ation, -ition	act or process	action, caution
-ible, -able	can be done	fixable, walkable
-al, -ial	having characteristics of	formal, natural
-y	characterized by	bloody, sunny
-ness	state of, condition of	kindness, darkness
-ity, -ty	state of	activity, loyalty
-ment	action or process	enjoyment, experiment
-ic	having characteristics of	strategic, logic
-ous, -eous, -ious	possessing the qualities of	joyous, nervous
-en	made of	golden, wooden
-er	comparative	smaller, happier
-ive, -ative, -itive	adjective form of noun	active, restive
-ful	full of	helpful, sorrowful
-less	without	headless, joyless
-est	comparative	smallest, sweetest

All other suffixes (approximately 160) account for only 3% of all the words containing suffixes.

Sources:

Blevins, W. (2001). *Teaching phonics and word study in the intermediate grades.* New York, NY: Scholastic.

Henry, M. (2003). *Unlocking literacy: Effective decoding and spelling instruction.* Baltimore, MD: Paul H. Brookes.

Yoshimoto, R. (1997). Phonemes, phonetics, and phonograms. *Teaching Exceptional Children, 29*(3), 43–47.

CHAPTER 4

Word Awareness Lessons

Word Detective

Materials
- Word Detective Magnifying Glass reproducible
- tagboard
- crayons or markers

Grade Levels

K–1

Objective

Students will increase attentiveness to spoken and written words, locate new words in conversation and reading, and use new words in speaking and writing.

 **Big Idea**

Background Information

Word consciousness is more than just knowledge of words. Students who are word conscious love words—they know words and use words often and well. Students who are aware of words understand the nuances of word meaning and know that words used correctly have the power to entertain, inform, and persuade. A good way to help students develop word awareness and the love of words is through word play. By creating an environment in which word learning is fun, students will be challenged and rewarded. "Word Detective" was created precisely for this purpose.

In advance, make a magnifying glass for each student and yourself using the **Word Detective Magnifying Glass reproducible (page 87)**. Reproduce the magnifying glasses on tagboard, cut them out (including the the "glass," so you are left with a frame), and have students decorate them with crayons or markers before the lesson.

Instructional Sequence

 1. Advance Organizer

Tell students:

Today we are going to play a game that will help you become aware of the words around you. If you look around, you will see that words are everywhere! People are talking all the time using words. Words are everywhere in print, too. For example, you see can see words on street signs, posters, and television.

Turn to a friend and tell him or her why you think it is important to understand words that you read or hear. I bet many of you mentioned that it is important to understand words so you can read stories. Did anyone mention that you need to be able to understand words so you can cook? Did anyone say that you need to be able to understand words so you can shop? Understanding words is so important!

When you play the game today, you will need to follow directions and listen carefully. After today, I will expect you to recognize words all around you and to begin to try and read them. Let's get started!

 2. Scaffolded Instruction

Model

Take students on a classroom tour. Start at a bulletin board and think aloud as you notice and read the words. Be dramatic and use your magnifying glass as you read. For example, you might say: *I am a word detective, and here are some words on the bulletin board. I'm going to read them. These words say* **Math Is Fun!** *Below the words, I see some of your math papers. These words tell us about your work and the fun you are having as you do it.*

Explain to students that as you play the game, you are going to ask them to investigate certain words and do the following:

- Repeat the word after you.

- Spell the word aloud.

- Think of a few sentences that include the word.

- Say what the word means.

Model the process with one of the words on the bulletin board. Discuss the importance of this word in the context in which it is written.

Do It With Me

Give each student his or her decorated magnifying glass. Then invite students to be word detectives. Continue the classroom tour. Choose specific words as you tour, and ask students to do the following:

- Repeat the word after you.

- Spell the word aloud.

- Think of a few sentences that include the word.

- Say what the word means.

On Your Own

Take the class into the hall or outside onto the school grounds. Form three groups of students. Be sure to group students of varying reading levels. Invite students to be word detectives and follow these steps to learn new words:

- Choose an interesting word.

- Read the word aloud.

- Repeat the word.

- Spell the word aloud.

- Think of a few sentences that include the word.

- Say what the word means.

 ## 3. Ongoing Practice

Keep students' magnifying glasses. From time to time, play "Word Detective" to help students become more aware of the words around them. Discuss the importance of the words as you study them.

Word Detective Magnifying Glass

Word Detour

Materials
- Word Detour reproducible
- thesaurus
- dry-erase boards

Grade Levels
2–3

Objective
Student will increase attentiveness to spoken and written words, locate new words in conversation and reading, and use new words in speaking and writing.

 **Big Idea**

Background Information
Word consciousness is more than just knowledge of words. Students who are word conscious love interesting, meaningful, and unique words—they know these words and use words often and well. Students who are aware of words understand that words used correctly have the power to entertain, inform, and persuade. Invite students to develop word awareness through activities that allow them to play with words. By creating an environment in which word learning is fun, students will be challenged and rewarded. "Word Detour" is an example of how to play with words and enhance students' vocabularies.

To prepare for the activity, copy a Word Detour sign for each student from the **Word Detour reproducible (page 91)**.

Instructional Sequence

 1. Advance Organizer

Tell students:

Today we are going to learn a game that will increase your vocabularies. Tell a partner what you know about vocabulary. What did your partner tell you? Does anyone have a different idea? **Vocabulary** *means the words you use and can understand when you read or hear someone speaking. It is called your* **lexicon**, *or the dictionary in your head.*

Use your dry-erase boards to write why you think we need to learn vocabulary. Being able to read is one reason to learn vocabulary. Another reason for learning vocabulary is that it helps you communicate. If you know a variety of words, you will be able to communicate your thoughts more clearly.

*We are going to play the "Word Detour" game. In this game, each of you will choose one word for all of us to avoid for a week. To find a "detour word," you must listen for a word that is overused and boring. Words like **walk**, **said**, **nice**, **very**, **hungry**, **tired**, and **bored** are overused words—we use them all the time, and there are much more interesting replacements for them! You must choose one overused word and find an interesting replacement for it. You will write the overused word and its replacement on a special sign and post it in the classroom. Once your sign is posted, no one can use the old word. We must all use the new word for a whole week. Let me show you how to get started.*

2. Scaffolded Instruction

Model

Use the words *tired* and *exhausted* to model the first week. Display the words on a Word Detour sign in the classroom.

Modeling Example *Let's imagine that I am assigned a detour word this week. I have noticed that most of you are saying **tired** a lot lately. I feel like I am constantly hearing, "I'm tired." There are more interesting words to use than **tired**, so I'm going to study a thesaurus and find one. Let's see. Here is the word **exhausted**. Let's fill out my Word Detour sign using the words **tired** and **exhausted**. Once I post my sign, you may not use the detour word **tired** anymore for a whole week. Instead, you must use the word **exhausted**. We must be aware of the words we are saying and hearing. If you hear someone use the detour word, let me know. We will keep a tally to see how many times we use the detour word and how many times we can use the new word instead. Do you think we can avoid the detour word for a whole week? Let's try!*

Do It With Me

Play "Word Detour" for a week with the words *tired* and *exhausted*, as explained in the Modeling Example. On the board, record tally marks to show how many times *tired* is used and how many times *exhausted* is used.

Name _____ Date _____

Word Detour

DETOUR
Do not use the word
tired

Use the word
exhausted

this week instead.

On Your Own

Every week, invite a student to replace one overused word with a new word. Encourage students to talk to adults, listen carefully to conversations, and ask for help when finding replacements for the overused words they choose.

3. Ongoing Practice

Post the Word Detour signs throughout the year in a long line. Once several replacement words are posted, you can play a word find game. Keep students actively engaged as you have them search for words in each of the following categories. Have students use dry-erase boards or work with partners. You might wish to award points or small prizes to the first pair who locates the word.

- Number of syllables (Example: *Find a word with four syllables.*)

- Word parts (Example: *Find a compound word.*)

- Meanings of word parts (Example: *Find a word with a prefix that means **not**.*)

- Spelling conventions (Example: *Find a word in which the **y** was changed to **i** before the suffix was added.*)

- Definition, synonym, or antonym (Example: *Find a word that is the opposite of **predictable**.*)

- Word in context (Example: *I can never tell what my sister will like to eat. One day she likes peas, and the next day she hates them. Her food tastes are _____.*)

Name _____   Date _____

Word Detour

DETOUR

Do not use the word

_____

Use the word

_____

this week
instead.

Word Hunt

Materials

- Word Hunt reproducible
- current student textbook
- teacher-made Levels of Word Knowledge rating scale poster
- dry-erase boards
- overhead projector and transparency

Grade Levels

2–3

Objective

Students will locate unfamiliar, challenging words while they read.

 **Big Idea**

Background Information

Word consciousness is interest in and knowledge of words, including their nuances and their power. Students who are aware of words know many words and use them often and well. Frequently, at-risk students do not notice unfamiliar words when they read. Sometimes the context gives enough information so the unknown word is not important to comprehension. Sometimes students become so engrossed in a story that they skip the unfamiliar words. At-risk readers need explicit strategies to become more aware of words and take the time to find out what they mean, whether in context, through using reference materials, or through word study. The following lesson helps students increase word awareness while reading so they can develop new vocabulary and become better readers, writers, listeners, and speakers.

Instructional Sequence

 1. Advance Organizer

Tell students:

Today you are going to learn how to pay attention to challenging words that you might skip when you read. Increasing your vocabulary is very important, and the best way to do that is by reading. But you must pay attention to challenging words. If you skip over them or ignore them, you will miss an opportunity to increase your vocabulary. You also might not understand what you read.

We have worked on challenging vocabulary words before. On your dry-erase boards, write what you think makes a word challenging. For example, a challenging word might be a word that you understand in one context but not in another.

In the past, I have selected vocabulary words, but this time you are going to find them while you read. You will need to hold a pencil in your

978-1-4129-5822-6

hand as you read and circle words that are challenging. After you find the words, you will record them.

After we play "Word Hunt," we will study these vocabulary words in other ways. Once you have read, written, and said the words several times through guided practice, I will expect you to use them correctly every day.

2. Scaffolded Instruction

Model

In advance, locate a textbook passage that contains a variety of challenging words. These words should be predominately Tier II words. Post a Levels of Word Knowledge rating scale poster that lists the criteria for evaluating word knowledge.

To begin, define what you mean by "challenging words," and tell students how many words you found in the passage that meet this criteria. Do not reveal the words.

Give students a copy of the **Word Hunt reproducible (page 95)**. Explain that they will use this sheet to record challenging words. Model how to read and locate the first challenging word. Hold a pencil and lightly circle the word. Show how to return to the text and record the circled word on the reproducible.

Demonstrate how to write the page number where the word was found and evaluate your level of knowledge using the Levels of Word Knowledge rating scale poster that you displayed. At this stage, do not define the word.

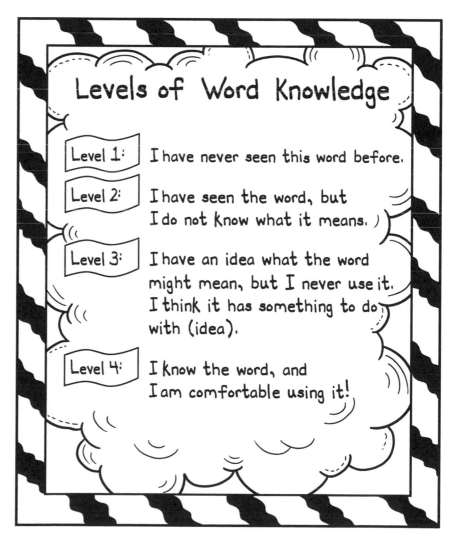

Levels of Word Knowledge

Level 1: I have never seen this word before.

Level 2: I have seen the word, but I do not know what it means.

Level 3: I have an idea what the word might mean, but I never use it. I think it has something to do with (idea).

Level 4: I know the word, and I am comfortable using it!

Do It With Me

Invite students to read the passage with you, find the next challenging word, circle it, and record the information on the Word Hunt reproducible.

Once you have completed the word, page number, and level of understanding for two sample words, work with students to define the words using context clues such as illustrations, photographs, and surrounding text. Record meanings in the last column on the reproducible. Check the meanings in the textbook's glossary or in a dictionary.

On Your Own

Have students continue reading and recording words, page numbers, and levels of understanding. Ask students to define three or four of the words. Afterward, display your word list on an overhead projector. Read through the words while students consult their papers. Invite volunteers to read aloud the words they defined as classmates record ideas on their reproducibles.

You might wish to award points for each word students found that matches your selection. If a student selects a word that is not on your list and can support why it meets the criteria, you might wish to award double points.

If you would like to determine a winner, have students keep a cumulative point total. The first student to earn a specific number of points is the winner. To reward all students without determining one winner, congratulate all those who meet or exceed the criterion number of points for that chapter.

3. Ongoing Practice

Complete "Word Hunts" throughout the year in several content areas. As you complete the lessons, add the new words to your selection of vocabulary words to study in-depth.

978-1-4129-5822-6

Name _____ Date _____

Word Hunt

Directions:
1. Find a challenging word from the text.
2. Record the word and the page number.
3. Decide on your level of understanding using the Rating Scale Key. Write **1**, **2**, **3**, or **4**.
4. Write a meaning for the word without using a dictionary. To find the meaning, use context clues: pictures, photos, and words and sentences around the word.

Rating Scale Key
Level 1: I have never seen this word before.
Level 2: I have seen the word, but I do not know what it means.
Level 3: I think I know the word.
Level 4: I know the word!

Word	Page Number	Level of Understanding	Meaning

References

Biemiller, A. (2003, Spring). Teaching vocabulary: Early, direct, sequential. *American Educator,* 143–148.

Blachowicz, C. L., Fisher, P. J., & Watts-Taffe, S. (2005). *Integrated vocabulary instruction: Meeting the needs of diverse learners in grades K–5.* Naperville, IL: Learning Point Associates.

Blevins, W. (2001). *Teaching phonics and word study in the intermediate grades.* New York, NY: Scholastic, Inc.

Chall, J., Jacobs, V., & Baldwin, L. E. (1990). *The reading crisis: Why poor children fall behind.* Cambridge, MA: Harvard University Press.

Cunningham, A., & Stanovich, K. (1997). Early reading acquisition and its relation to reading experience and ability ten years later. *Developmental Psychology, 33,* 934–945.

Feldman, K., & Kinsella, K. (2002). *Narrowing the gap: The case for explicit vocabulary instruction.* New York, NY: Scholastic, Inc.

Frayer, D., Frederick, W. C., & Klausmeier, H. J. (1960). *A schema for testing the level of concept mastery.* (Working Paper No. 16). Madison, WI: University of Wisconsin.

Graves, M. F. (1986). Vocabulary learning and instruction. In E. Z. Rothkopf & L. C. Ehri (Eds.) *Review of research in education, Vol. 13* (pp. 49–89). Washington, DC: American Educational Research Association.

Henry, M. (2003). *Unlocking literacy: Effective decoding and spelling instruction.* Baltimore, MD: Paul H. Brookes.

Hickman, P., Pollard-Durodola, S., & Vaugh, S. (2004). Storybook reading: Improving vocabulary and comprehension for English language learners. *The Reading Teacher 57*(8), 720–730.

Jintendra, A., & Kameeniu, E. J. (1994). A review of the concept learning models: Implications for special education practitioners. *Intervention in School and Clinic, 30*(2), 91–98.

Levin, J. R., Dretzke, B. J., Pressley, M., & McGivern, J. E. (1985). In search of the keyword method/vocabulary comprehension link. *Contemporary Educational Psychology, 10,* 220–227.

Lima, C. (2006). *A to zoo: Subject access to children's picture books* (7th ed.). Westport, CN: Libraries Unlimited.

McEwan, E. K. (2002). *Teach them all to read: Catching the kids who fall through the cracks.* Thousand Oaks, CA: Corwin Press.

Moats, L. (2001, Summer). *Overcoming the language gap.* Retrieved December 19, 2005, from the American Educator Web site: http://www.aft.org/pubs-reports/american_educator/summer2001/lang_gap_moats.html.

Nagy, W., & Anderson, R. C. (1984). How many words are there in printed school English? *Reading Research Quarterly, 19,* 304–330.

National Reading Panel. (2000). *Teaching children to read: An evidence-based assessment of the scientific research literature on reading and its implications for reading instruction.* Bethseda, MD: National Institutes of Health.

Santa, C., Havens, L., & Valdes, B. (2004). *Project CRISS: Creating independence through student owned strategies* (3rd ed.). Dubuque, IA: Kendall/Hunt Publishing Company.

Stahl, S. A. (2003, Spring). *Words are learned incrementally over multiple exposures.* Retrieved November 25, 2006, from the American Educator Web site: http://www.aft.org/pubs-reports/american_educator/spring2003/stahl.html.

Wallis, C., & Steptoe, S. (2006). How to bring our schools out of the 20th century. *Time Magazine, 168*(25), 50–56.

978-1-4129-5822-6